BORDERLANDS

BORDERLANDS

new photographs and old tales
of the sacred springs, holy wells and spas
of Cheshire, Flintshire, Denbighshire, Shropshire, Worcestershire,
Radnorshire, Herefordshire, Breconshire, Montgomeryshire,
Monmouthshire and Gloucestershire

PHIL COPE

with poems by
RS Thomas, Graham Hartill, William Shakespeare, Caroline Carver, Charlotte Wardle, AE Housman, Wilfred Owen
Mary Webb, Felicia Hemans, TS Eliot, John Webster, Francis Brett Young, Gillian Clarke, Robert Minhinnick, Einion Wan
Bleddyn Fardd, Gruffudd ab yr Ynad Coch, Dafydd Llwyd ap Llywelyn ap Gruffudd, Ruth Bidgood, and Bob Dylan

Seren
is the book imprint of
Poetry Wales Press Ltd
Nolton Street, Bridgend, Wales

01656 663 018
www.serenbooks.com
facebook.com/SerenBooks
twitter: @SerenBooks

© Phil Cope, 2013

The right of Phil Cope to be identified
as the Author of this Work has been asserted
in accordance with the Copyright,
Designs and Patents Act, 1988.

ISBN 978-1-78172-060-8

A CIP record for this title is available
from the British Library.

All rights reserved.
No part of this publication may be
reproduced, stored in a retrieval system,
or transmitted at any time
or by any means electronic,
mechanical, photocopying, recording
or otherwise without the prior permission
of the copyright holders.

The publisher works with the financial
assistance of the Welsh Books Council.

Designed for Seren by
Phil Cope, culture & democracy
phil.cope@talktalk.net

Printed in the Czech Republic
by Akcent Media Ltd.

contents

Location Map		8
Introduction: a geography of difference		11

In Search of Ripples from Pre-Christian Sacred Springs — 19

The Wizard's Well	Alderley Edge, near Wilmslow, Cheshire	22
The Holy Well	Alderley Edge, Cheshire	23
The Wishing Well	Alderley Edge, Cheshire	24
St Thomas' Holy Well	near Llanveynoe, Olchon Valley, Herefordshire	25
St John the Baptist Holy Well	Hope Bagot, near Ludlow, Shropshire	29
St Peter's Well	Peterchurch, Herefordshire	33
Ffynnon Elian	Llanelian, near Colwyn Bay, Denbighshire	34
Ffynnon Degla	Llandegla, near Ruthin, Denbighshire	38
Depplewell	Depple Wood, Moccas, near Bredwardine, Herefordshire	40
St Ann's Well	Aconbury, near Hereford, Herefordshire	43
The Virtuous Well	Trellech, near Monmouth, Monmouthshire	43
Havelock Well	Much Wenlock, Shropshire	47

The Fine Art of Bathing in Roman Britain — 49

Viroconium Cornoviorum	Wroxeter, near Shrewsbury, Shropshire	53
Isca Augusta	Caerleon, Monmouthshire	60
Noden's Temple	Lydney Park, Dwarf Hill, Lydney, Forest of Dean, Gloucestershire	63
Venta Silurum	Caerwent, Monmouthshire	64
Balineae Silures	Castell Collen, near Llandrindod Wells, Radnorshire / Powys	68
Prestatyn Bath House	Melyd Avenue, Prestatyn, Denbighshire	71
New Weir Water Shrine	Weir Gardens, Swainshill, Herefordshire	72

Holy Wells in the Age of the Saints — 75

Our Lady Well	Hempsted, near Gloucester, Gloucestershire	79
Mary's Well	Bodrhyddan Hall, near Rhuddlan, Denbighshire	80
Ffynnon Fair	Llanfair Ceireinion, Montgomeryshire / Powys	82
Ffynnon Fair	near Trefnant, near St Asaph, Denbighshire	84
St Anthony's Well	Edgehills Plantation, near Cinderford, Forest of Dean, Glous.	88
St Julian(a)'s Well	Ludlow, Shropshire	90
The Holy Well of St Dubricious	Hentland, near Ross-on-Wye, Herefordshire	93
Ffynnon Gybi	Llangybi, near Newport, Monmouthshire	97
St Ethelbert's Well	St Mary's Church, Marden, near Hereford, Herefordshire	100
St Ethelbert's Well	Castle Green, Hereford, Herefordshire	101

St Winefride's Well	Holywell, Flintshire	106
St Winefride's Well	Woolston, near Oswestry, Shropshire	110
Ffynnon Beuno	Tremeirchion, near St Asaph, Denbighshire	114
Ffynnon Beuno	Gwyddelwern, near Corwen, Denbighshire	115
Wenlock Priory	Much Wenlock, Shropshire	117
St Milburga's Well	Stoke St Milborough, Shropshire	121
St Milburga's Well	Much Wenlock, Shropshire	122
Ffynnon Gynhafal	Llangynhafal, near Ruthin, Denbighshire	122
St Chad's Well	Chadkirk, Romiley, near Stockport	127
St Chad's Well	Lichfield, Staffordshire	128
Lichfield Cathedral	Lichfield, Staffordshire	129
St Kenelm's Well	near Romsley, Clent Hills, Worcestershire	134
St Kenelm's Well	near Winchcombe, Sudeley Hill, near Cheltenham, Gloucestershire	137
Winchcombe Abbey	Winchcombe, Gloucestershire	141

Holy Wells in the Age of the Warrior Princes — 145

St Tewdrig's Well	Mathern, near Chepstow, Monmouthshire	146
St Oswald's Well	Heritage Green, Winwick, near Warrington, Cheshire	148
St Oswald's Well	Maserfield, Oswestry, Shropshire	151
St Oswald's Well	Holywell, Flintshire	152
Strata Florida	Pontrhydfendigaid, near Tregaron, Ceredigion	154
Llywelyn ap Gruffydd's Well	Cilmeri, near Builth Wells, Radnorshire / Powys	160
Abbey Cwm Hir	near Llandrindod Wells, Radnorshire / Powys	162
Abergavenny Castle	Abergavenny, Monmouthshire	163
Sycharth Castle	Llansilin, Montgomeryshire / Powys	164
Glyndyfrdwy Mound	near Llangollen, Denbighshire	165
St Mary's Well	Pilleth, near Knighton, Radnorshire / Powys	167
Bronllys Castle Well	near Talgarth, Breconshire / Powys	171
Beeston Castle Wells	Tarporley, Cheshire	174
Ludlow Castle Wells	Castle Square, Ludlow, Shropshire	176
Stokesay Castle Well	near Craven Arms, Shropshire	178
Raglan Castle Wells	Raglan, Monmouthshire	181

A New Fashion for Spas — 185

Trefriw Spa	Trefriw, near Betws-y-Coed, Conwy	187
Droitwich Spa	Droitwich, Worcestershire	189
Nantwich	Cheshire	192

Northwich	Cheshire	193
Llandrindod Wells	Radnorshire / Powys	194
Cheltenham Spa	Cheltenham, Gloucestershire	201
Tenbury Wells	Malvern Hills, Worcestershire	204
Walm's Well	News Wood, Malvern Hills, near Ledbury, Herefordshire	210
St Ann's Well	Great Malvern, Worcestershire	211
Holy Well	Malvern Wells, Worcestershire	215
Earl Beauchamp's Fountain	Malvern Hills, Worcestershire	217
Evendine Spring	Brand Green, Malvern Hills, Worcestershire	219
Hospital Fountain	Malvern Hills, Worcestershire	220
Hay Slad Spout	Malvern Hills, Worcestershire	222
Westminster Bank Spout	Malvern Hills, Worcestershire	223
The Clock Tower / Water Tank	North Malvern, Worcestershire	224
Enigma Fountain	Great Malvern, Worcestershire	231
Malvhina Fountain	Great Malvern, Worcestershire	232

Holy Wells into the Twenty-First Century   235

Sutton Hills Hillfort Well	Sutton St Michael, near Marden, Herefordshire	236
The Old Bridge Well	Llanfyllin, Mongomeryshire / Powys	237
Whistlebitch Well	near Utkinton, Cheshire	238
Billy Hobby's Well	Grosvenor Park Wells, Chester, Cheshire	240
Jacob's Well	Grosvenor Park Wells, Chester, Cheshire	241
Cleobury Mortimer Wells	Cleobury Mortimer, Shropshire	241
Llanwrtyd Wells	Radnorshire / Powys	242
Llangammarch Wells	nr Builth Wells, Breconshire / Powys	245
Ffynnon Ddyfnog	Llanrhaeadr-yng-Nghinmeirch, Denbighshire	246
Venta Silurum	Caerwent, Monmouthshire	249

A Few Last Words   251

Index of Sites   254

Acknowledgements   254

Selected Further Reading   255

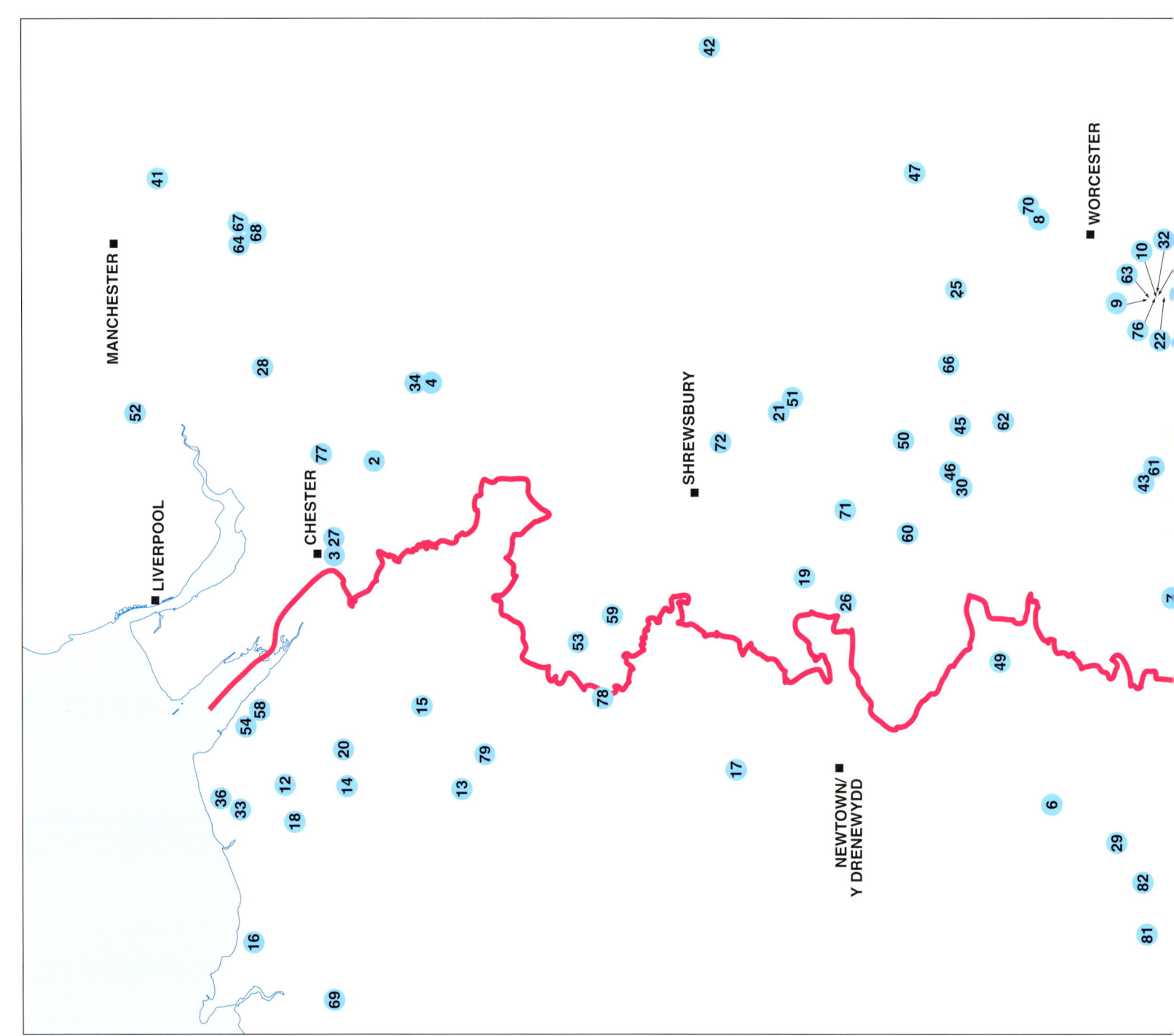

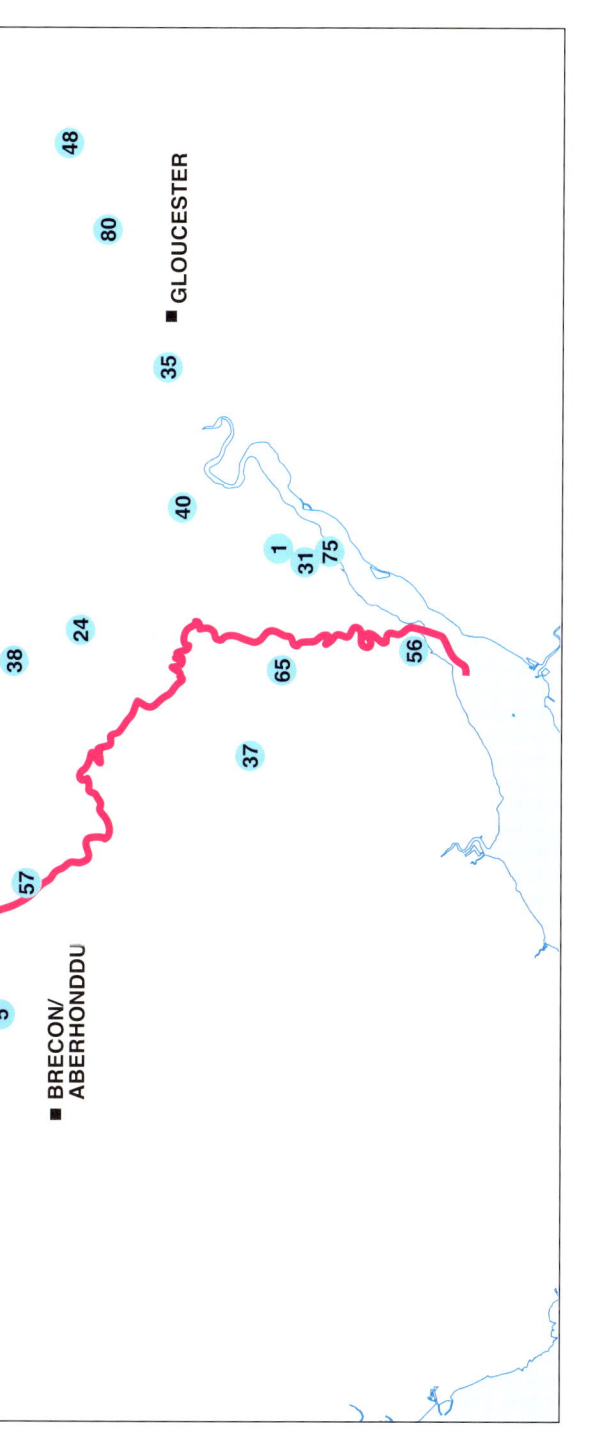

1. Balineae Silures 68
2. Beaston Castle 174
3. Billy Hobby's Well 240
4. Brine Spring 192
5. Bronllys Castle 171
6. Llandrindod Wells 194
7. Depplewell 40
8. Droitwich Spa Lido 189
9. Earl Beauchamp's Fountain 217
10. Enigma Fountain 231
11. Evendine Spring 219
12. Ffynnon Beuno, Tremeirchion 114
13. Ffynnon Beuno, Gwyddelwern 115
14. Ffynnon Ddyfnog 246
15. Ffynnon Degla 38
16. Ffynnon Elian 34
17. Ffynnon Fair, Llanfair Caereinion 82
18. Ffynnon Fair, Trefnant 84
19. Ffynnon Gybi 97
20. Ffynnon Gynhafal 122
21. Havelock Well 47
22. Hay Slad Spout 222
23. Holy Well 215
24. Holy Well of St Dubricious 93
25. Hospital Fountain 220
26. Isca Augusta 60
27. Jacob's Well 241
28. Lion Salt Works 194
29. Llywelyn ap Gruffydd Well 160
30. Ludlow Castle 176
31. Lydney Park Roman Temple 63
32. Malvhina Fountain 232
33. Mary's Well 80
34. Old Biot 192
35. Our Lady Well 79
36. Prestatyn Roman Bath House 71
37. Raglan Castle 181
38. St Ann's Well 43
39. St Anne's Well 211
40. St Anthony's Well 88
41. St Chad's Well. Chadkirk 127
42. St Chad's Well. Lichfield 128
43. St Ethelbert's Well, Marden 100
44. St Ethelbert's Well, Castle Green 101
45. St John the Baptist Holy Well 29
46. St Julian's Well 90
47. St Kenelm's Well, Romsley 134
48. St Kenelm's Well, Winchcombe 137
49. St Mary's Well 167
50. St Milburga's Well, Stoke St Milburga 121
51. St Milburga's Well, Much Wenlock 122
52. St Oswald's Well, Winwick 148
53. St Oswald's Well, Maserfield 151
54. St Oswald's Well, Holywell 152
55. St Peter's Well 33
56. St Tewdrig's Well 146
57. St Thomas's Well 25
58. St Winefride's Well, Holywell 106
59. St Winefride's Well, Woolston 110
60. Stokesay Castle 178
61. Sutton Wells Hillfort 236
62. Tenbury Wells Pump Rooms 204
63. The Clock Tower Well 224
64. The Holy Well 24
65. The Virtuous Well 43
66. Cleobury Mortimer wells 24
67. The Wishing Well 23
68. The Wizard's Well 22
69. Trefriw Spa 187
70. Upwich Brine Pit 190
71. Venta Silurum 64
72. Viroconium Cornoviorum 53
73. Walm's Well 210
74. Weir Gardens, Swainshill 72
75. Wenlock Priory 117
76. Westminster Bank Spout 223
77. Whistlebitch Well 238
78. Sycarth Castle 164
79. Glyndyfrdwy Mound 165
80. Cheltenham Spa 201
81. Llanwrtyd Wells 242
82. Llangammarch Wells 245

BORDERLANDS

Offa's Dyke, near Garbett Hall, Knighton, Radnorshire / Powys

INTRODUCTION
a geography of difference

It is exciting to walk the very edge of things, whether it is a cliff top or an idea.

David Adam, *Border Lands*, 1991

The Wales / England Borderlands are infused by the turbulent and bloody history of our struggles to define who we are and how we should live, on either side of a constantly-disputed front line. Invaded and settled in turn by Celtic tribes, and by Roman legions, by Angles, Saxons and by Normans, the area offers one of the world's richest tapestries of conflict, of oppression and rebellion, where the results are still starkly illustrated in the landscape in a plethora of mounds, forts and castles, and the sites of countless battles.

But, as well as providing the rolling combat zone for conventional armies of the past, the border that runs roughly between Chester in the north and Chepstow in the south has been, and in many ways still is a major arena for the battle of ideas … around Celtic and Anglo-Saxon values, paganism and Christianity (as well as various versions of Christianity, itself), the spiritual and the materialistic, the poetic and the prosaic, as well as around our different languages.

It is not insignificant that 'Welsh', the name the Saxons gave to the native inhabitants, means 'strangers', and 'Cymry', the word the Britons used to describe themselves, means 'people of the same land' or 'the land of comrades'. England, on the other hand, was described by a ninth century Welsh poet as 'tir trahawg', the arrogant country. The right to belong in the Borderlands then was clearly a cultural as well as a military undertaking.

A clearly-delineated border provides protection from 'barbarians' – however we may wish to define them – as well as a gathering place for attack. And it also offers the possibility for co-operation, for connections with the other, for the broadening of minds and the softening of hearts. Borders are places to defend and from which to exclude the outsider, to draw your line in the sand; as well as offering neutral places at which to meet, to mingle and to exchange views on the world; places at which to offer ultimatums as well as to find compromise and friendship.

To live within the Wales / England Borderlands is always to have views in two distinct directions, one towards the rational, business-like and forward-looking Anglo-Saxon world, the other to the passionate and poetic Wales, given always, it seems, to extremes and ever-willing to live within the fading light of past glories (and the kind of stereotyping that RS Thomas and I are regularly in danger of perpetuating):

Welsh Landscape

To live in Wales is to be conscious
At dusk of the spilled blood
That went to the making of the wild sky,
Dyeing the immaculate rivers
In all their courses.
It is to be aware,
Above the noisy tractor
And hum of the machine
Of strife in the spring woods,
Vibrant with sped arrows.
You cannot live in the present,
At least not in Wales.
There is the language for instance,
The soft consonants
Strange to the ear.
There are cries in the dark at night
As owls answer the moon,
And thick ambush of shadows,
Hushed at the fields' corners.
There is no present in Wales,
And no future;
There is only the past,
Brittle with relics,
Wind-bitten towers and castles
With sham ghosts;
Mouldering quarries and mines;
And an impotent people,
Sick with inbreeding,
Worrying the carcass of an old song.

RS Thomas

BORDERLANDS

Cross Well, Robinswood Hill, Gloucester

St Peter's Well, Peterchurch, Herefordshire

Another poet, **Graham Hartill,** who was born in the industrial West Midlands but moved to study, work and live in Wales from the early 1970s onwards, explores his own journey in his poem 'The View West':

The lane between the houses opposite
(white council houses,
built 2 years after the War)
heading west
into a field,
  a further field,
a pond, a stile,
  the blue hills of Shropshire
west, beyond –

a line straight out of the terrain behind:
the limestone ridge
that birthed colossal industry
  from ancient deposits,
woodland
  set on fire –
it was everything
     melting and hardening,
  that world

I went west
for the supple myths of mountains
and a land
looking soft and blue,
that's what you do
     or don't do

  dropped on the edge

As much as anything else, it was geography that helped create and secure our two nations' separatenesses.

The land here represented much more than a place to settle, to farm and to multiply; it fed the nurturing roots of our identities, as if our cultural DNA was contained within the mountains and the valleys and the streams.

This is an area where some rivers on their journeys to the sea repeatedly change nationality, while others actually draw our boundary lines, their waters sharing nations, with each bank flying a different flag. And, more than anything else, it is our mountain geography that has provided the most obvious physical barrier between the English and the Welsh people, a rocky barricade to the complete over-running of the ancient British nation and its language:

The English may have won the prosperous valleys and glens: but the Welsh secretly took the real prize – to live in the uplands, on the bright hill under the black cloud, their proximity to God and to heaven alike guaranteed henceforth by nothing less than the landscape itself.

Peter J Conradi
*At the Bright Hem of God:
Radnorshire Pastoral,* 2009

the first boundaries

It was customary for the English to cut off the ears of every Welshman who was found to the east of the dyke, and for the Welsh to hang every Englishman whom they found to the west of it.

George Borrow, *Wild Wales*, 1862

Although the old Brythonic kingdom of the Celts – which lent its name to modern Britain – stretched far beyond the present border (as far north at its height as the Firth of Forth), the first significant boundary between what we now know as England and Wales was the military highway built by the Romans between their chain of forts from *Isca* (Caerleon) in the south and *Deva* (Chester) in the north, in the first centuries of the Modern Era. The second and most famous, perhaps, the 'Dyke' of the Mercian King Offa, was constructed between the estuaries of the rivers Dee and Severn in the eighth century to resist Welsh attack.

From the late eleventh century onwards, new, even more elaborate ways to demonstrate who was in charge and what was and was not now permitted were introduced during the first major period of castle building in what came to be known as the Welsh Marches (from *marca*, the Latin word for 'border'), following the Norman Conquest of 1066.

Caerleon Roman baths

Offa's Dyke path at Penycleddiau Mound, Clwydian Range

The Welsh were denied access to most of these fortresses, and severely punished if found within their walls. The loss of an arm or even death awaited those who crossed the line. In the twelfth century, the Lord of Clun offered a reward to anyone who brought him the skin of "a wild Welshman".

It is ironic, then, that many of our most impressive physical monuments in Wales – our great castles, and our church and monastic buildings upon which much of our tourist industry is based – are the products of oppression, constructed by Marcher Lord or Benedictine monk, to undermine local power or belief, "a magnificent symbol" in the words of Thomas Pennant (1726-1798) "of our subjection".

borderlands to another world

The struggles to define the contested territories of the Wales / England Borderlands were reflected in the explanations of the true meanings of our springs and of our wells, similarly set within a permanent battlefield of interpretations, constantly changing over time. Many ancient traditions included the belief that sacred springs issued from a supernatural underworld, the spiritual womb of Mother Earth, before flowing through the lands' rivers to the sea.

BORDERLANDS

Raglan Castle, Monmouthshire

Celtic mythology places the Well of Wisdom at the very centre of its Otherworld, the spiritual source from which all waters, and life itself, was created.

In pre-Christian times, water appearing unaided and unbidden from the hard rock or the dry soil of the earth's belly, would have had a magical significance for our ancestors, not only as an element essential to all life but, just as importantly, as a place where the most powerful of nature spirits resided and where a dialogue with other realities was possible, "borderland places" in the words of Janet and Colin Bord, "where this world and the hidden Otherworld meet". (*Sacred Waters: Holy Wells and Water Lore in Britain and Ireland*, 1985)

above: Hay Slad, Malvern Hills, Worcestershire

opposite: the Rotunda Montpellier (once a pump and ball room, now a bank), Cheltenham Spa

These potential portals to another reality grew into centres for elaborate ceremonies and ritual, for story-telling and the presenting of gifts, in return for which the waters could offer the favours of good health, love and fertility. Some wells predicted and sometimes even influenced the future, while others could even be used to lay curses.

When the Romans arrived on these shores, they brought with them a new bath house culture, and a range of alternative water deities and spirits which were regularly married with their local equivalents. Christian missionaries to Britain initially recognised the powers of these sites to sustain and to inspire, also giving them new names and allying them to new legends while essentially retaining their original meanings for ordinary people. It was clear that incorporation rather than destruction of these pagan truths was the only viable option.

It was not until the Protestant Reformation of the second half of the sixteenth century that the church decided to undertake a wholesale obliteration of the water cult sites and their beliefs, although thankfully, this, as we shall see, was never fully achieved.

Then, in the eighteenth century, the invasion of science offered a further layer of explanation with the development of the lucrative spa movement in Britain.

BORDERLANDS

And today, water is still big business and a renewed interest in sources of clean, unadulterated springs and the tales which have added to their attraction, seems to be developing once again as we watch while nature groans under the weight of our greed and more than a billion people worldwide lack a regular and safe supply.

On the Borderlands running directly north-south between England and Wales, we can look both west or east along a broad line of myth and history, but when arriving at one of the very many well sites still to be found within this legendary corridor, we are forced to look downwards, into their waters and simultaneously up to their reflections of a moving sky.

These special places encourage us gently to move from the everyday a little way towards the extraordinary, and on a good day even, from the earthly perhaps to the potentially sacred.

Malvhina Fountain, Great Malvern, Worcestershire

notes on the structure of *Borderlands*

This – my third major volume on the sacred springs, holy wells and spas of Britain published by Seren – explores a selection of just 94 of the very many Borderlands wells I have studied and photographed over the past ten years. Although I have tried to offer an historical overview of all of the aspects of the sites in the area, my main motivation is not that of the historian; it is rather, to capture something of the spirit and the beauty – so often, unfortunately, hidden and neglected – of these important places.

The structure of this volume is led, then, first and foremost by my photographs, presented in a loose chronology which offered me a convenient ordering of the images from prehistory, through the contributions the Romans made to sacred water lore in Britain, through the ages of the saints and of the princes, then on through the spa movement to arrive at an examination of the state of well culture today.

Some may feel that an important site essential to the story is omitted, a result, perhaps, of the inadequacy of my research and/or the size restrictions of a single volume. The process of selection was a difficult one, resulting inevitably in the discarding of some powerful images and stories. My intenton, however, was not merely to provide records of these special places, but to connect visually, narratively and spiritually with each site, to capture something of its truth through time, at these unusual places where heaven and earth are believed to have touched.

and thanks

In thanking the following people who have assisted me in providing both direct and indirect support to this Borderlands project – in writing and publishing essential works which I have dipped into in my research, in suggesting sites I may have overlooked, in offering words of inspiration or of warning, or in questioning my notions and even checking my style - it must be stressed that the conclusions I come to and the mistakes I make are mine alone:

Angela Graham, Jane Beckerman, Stephen Thomas, Rev Andrew E Morton, Miss Paddy Willis, Ruth Buckley, Tristan Gray Hulse, Vanessa Horne, Laura Cope, Dewi Roberts, Dawn Worgan (clerk, Tenbury Town Council), Janet Bord, John R. Love (chairman, Llangybi Fawr Community Council), Charles and Jan Kenchington, Mike Rust, Bruce Osborne and Cora Weaver.

And, if the following apology from Shakespeare's *Henry V* for the limits of the playwright's historical knowledge is good enough for him, then it's good enough for me:

Vouchsafe to those that have not read the story,

That I may prompt them; and of such that have,

I humbly pray them to admit the excuse

Of time, of numbers, and due course of things

Which cannot in their huge and proper life

Be here presented …

DEITIES TO BE FEARED AND LOVED
in search of ripples from pre-christian sacred springs

It is all part of a wider magic, hud *in Welsh, which is really a key to life and matter itself – the sense that the divine resides in everything around us.... The sacred oak-groves of the Celts, the intuitive nature-poems of medieval lyricists, the imagery of the folklore, all attest to this ancient instinct, which gave sanctity to the land itself, and made the days full of wonder.*

Jan Morris, *Wales, Epic Views of a Small Country*, 1984

Sacred springs which have their origins in a time before Christianity arrived on these shores are not easy to find along the Wales / England borders, an area where tides of change have repeatedly swept over the land, taking from and adding to the oldest geographies of belief.

We have inherited no written records from our earliest ancestors, so we are left to piece together the picture of their lives through the often unreliable accounts of their adversaries, as well as from the few pieces of material evidence we have managed to unearth in their carvings, jewellery and pottery fragments, and their much larger constructions in the landscape.

And some faint glimmerings of waters which suggest an older pattern of thinking and the neglected practices which supported it at a time when all nature was supernatural, are still sometimes visible, though always well-hidden beneath layers of change.

... the water-spirits of primaeval mythology are as souls which cause the water's rush and rest, its kindness and its cruelty... man finds in the beings which, with such power, can work him weal and woe, deities to be feared and loved ...

Dr Edward Burnett Tylor (1832-1917), *Primitive Culture*, 1871

opposite: St Thomas's Well, Llanveynoe, Herefordshire

above: Fynnon Fair, Trefnant, Denbighshire

on the edge

Alderley Edge near Wilmslow in Cheshire is a steep and thickly-wooded red sandstone escarpment which overlooks the Cheshire Plain. The area is steeped in a history that seems to seep from its stones and its trees.

There is evidence of people lving here since the Mesolithic period (around 10,000 BC) and of an extensive copper mining industry in the Bronze Age (from 2,500 BC) at the very dawn of our experimentation with the fashioning of metals in our search for food, in the construction of our weapons of war, and for bodily adornment. And in 1995, members of the Derbyshire Caving Club discovered a hoard of 564 Roman coins here dating from 317 AD.

This is an area of ancient sacred waters, numerous caves and dark tunnels, a storehouse of precious metals … and of stories hidden deep within its rocks.

left: the Wishing Well, Alderley Edge

opposite the face and the words of the wizard, Wizard's Well, Alderley Edge

One tale – used by local author Alan Garner as the inspiration for his two early fantasy novels, *The Weirdstone of Brisingamen* and *The Moon of Gomrath* – tells of a secret cavern in the dense forest on the Edge, guarded by an ancient wizard (some say Merlin), within which sleeps an army of ageless knights (some say led by Arthur) dressed in silver armour and ready to be called at a time of peril for the people of Britain. And all of the knights – except one – have powerful steeds, saddled and ready for action.

The story tells that on one fateful day this Alderley Edge wizard sees a farmer taking his white mare to market, and asks him if he can buy the animal.

The farmer, thinking he can attract a better price at the fair in Macclesfield, declines his offer and continues on his way, despite the wizard's confident declaration that no one will show any interest in the horse.

The old man's prediction comes true and, on the farmer's return, he makes the offer a second time. Tired and penniless, the farmer gladly accepts and the wizard instructs him to follow him deeper into the forest.

At a place known locally as Stormy Point, the wizard bangs the ground with his stick.

To the farmer's great surprise, the rocks open up to reveal a pair of splendidly-decorated iron gates.

The wizard takes the farmer and his mare through the gates and deep into the cavern where the knights are sleeping. The place is stacked high with precious stones, with gold and silver coins and other treasures, and the wizard invites his visitor to help himself as payment for the horse. The grateful farmer fills his arms and quickly makes for the cave's exit, soon finding himself back in the woods, alone once again.

It was reported that, on very many occasions after his magical ordeal, the farmer searched the woodlands of the Edge to find the cavern's entrance and the magical iron gates, but failed each time.

Given the geology of the area, it is no surprise that there are such a large number of ancient springs on Alderley Edge. And it's clear from the many remains found here of our earliest ancestors that the water from these springs would have been an important determinant of these earliest settlements … as well as a powerful backdrop for the development of myths and legends to help explain their confusing world.

The Wizard's Well

Alderley Edge
near Wilmslow, Cheshire
OS Explorer Map No.268:
SJ 855 780

... the children came upon a stone trough into which water was dripping from an overhanging cliff, and high in the rock was carved the face of a bearded man, and underneath was engraved:

DRINK OF THIS
AND TAKE THY FILL
FOR THE WATER FALLS
BY THE WIZARD'S WILL

from *The Weirdstone of Brisingamen* by **Alan Garner**

It is claimed that the carving of these words at the Wizard's Well was made around two hundred years ago by local stone mason, Robert Garner, the novelist Alan Garner's great-great grandfather, although the face of the wizard is thought to be very much older.

The Holy Well

Alderley Edge, Cheshire
OS Explorer Map No.268:
SJ 859 779

According to one source, both wells (Wizard and Holy) "were in ancient times connected with well worship. Their healing powers were considered to be unfailing: the barren, the blind, the lame, and bodily-afflicted constantly made their way thither; maidens whispered their vows and prayers over them, their lovers and their future lives being their theme. Some of the sex deposit the pins in their straight and original form, others bend them only at right angle, and as many again seem to consider the charm alone to act effectively when carefully and conscientiously doubled-up."

(C Roeder and FS Graves
Recent Archaeological Discoveries at Alderley Edge, 1905)

opposite: Wizard's Well, Alderley Edge and The Wizard of Edge Inn

right: Holy Well, Alderley Edge

BORDERLANDS

The Wishing Well
Alderley Edge, Cheshire
OS Explorer Map No.268:
SJ 860 777

This beautifully evocative site next to a hollow created most probably by early miners in search of copper ores, is said to promise seven years bad luck for passersby who fail to re-place a rhododendron leaf in the rock fissure to allow the water to fall into the deep carved basin below.

left: Alderley Edge
above: the Wishing Well

opposite: a pilgrim at St Thomas' Sacred Spring
(during a guided tour led by the author
for the Breddfa Centre, May 2012)

a site for sore eyes

St Thomas' Holy Well
near Llanveynoe, Olchon Valley, Herefordshire
OS Outdoor Leisure Map No.13: SO 284 320

This Olchon Valley sacred spring near Llanveynoe on the Herefordshire / Monmouthshire border is – despite its re-dedication to St Thomas – one of those rare places which retains something of the spirit and atmosphere of pre-Christian well culture.

The water which emerges from under a rock, shaded by two trunks of a huge shading tree, fills a small pool before running down to the river below in this most contemplative of sites

Traditionally, the spring was used by those suffering from rheumatism and with weak eyes, and still today there is evidence of visitors seeking its medicinal as well as its metaphysical comforts.

BORDERLANDS

The Olchon Valley is a spiritually-charged area which has attracted pilgrims from a variety of denominations for millennia. It is believed that St Beuno came here in the early seventh century, and inside his nearby church can be found two early Christian stones, one of which shows a crucifixion scene overlaying pagan cup marks, suggesting the christianisation of a much earlier monument.

And, in the churchyard, there is an impressive short-armed pre-Conquest cross with an unusual water channel groove running down its back, pointing perhaps to yet another act of aesthetic and religious recycling.

right: evidence of the continuing usage of Llanveynoe's sacred waters

right: one of the ancient carved stones set into the wall inside St Beuno's Church, Llanveynoe

below: St Beuno's Church, Llanveynoe, built in the thirteenth century, and the unusual cross in the graveyard (OS Outdoor Leisure Map No.13: SO 303 314)

PRE-CHRISTIAN SACRED SPRINGS

the green man

St John the Baptist Holy Well

Hope Bagot, near Ludlow, Shropshire
OS Explorer Map No.203:
SO 589 741

The area around the well at Hope Bagot in Shropshire – today re-dedicated to St John the Baptist – also has, like that at Llanveynoe, a palpable sense of timeless spirituality. Though little is really know of the history of this site, there is compelling evidence of pre-Christian and early Christian usage here.

Sitting directly above the well is an enormous yew tree, at least 1,600 years old, and packed with contemporary pagan garlands and offerings.

Trees have offered a powerful focus for religious life for people in every part of the world from earliest times, an elaborate mythology of beliefs supporting a wide range of arboreal cults at these sacred groves. It is claimed by some that the title of Druid derives from words for 'knowledge of the oak'.

opposite: the giant yew tree, Hope Bagot

above: stained glass window of John baptising Jesus, St John the Baptist Church, Hope Bagot

BORDERLANDS

Green Man

As he sprang from the ground
he was covered with leaves
his head shook with scorn
his arms had no hands.

When we saw he was there
he was seven feet high
now his eyes watch us.

I made sure he had roots
before I went near
heard his breath catch
as if he were laughing.

Last night there were storms
rains lashed at the trees
whipped the young saplings

but the Green Man grows stronger
no birds sit in his branches
I swear he moves closer.

Soon it will be May
and the full moon will burst
sprinkling her light
like dew on the grass.

He is old as she is
her wax will coat him in frail light
bring him fully awake

I fear the morning
he strips his roots
leaps from the earth
to waste the countryside

Caroline Carver

PRE-CHRISTIAN SACRED SPRINGS

As well as the tree and the sacred spring directly below it at Hope Bagot, the site offers two further connections to a possible pagan past.

The walls of the churchyard here are circular, usually a sign of pre-Christian origins. And, in addition, a pair of stone heads have been cemented into the walls above the porch, confirmed in 1995 as "pre-Roman Iron Age or of the Romano-British period" by the School of History and Archaeology at the University of Wales Cardiff.

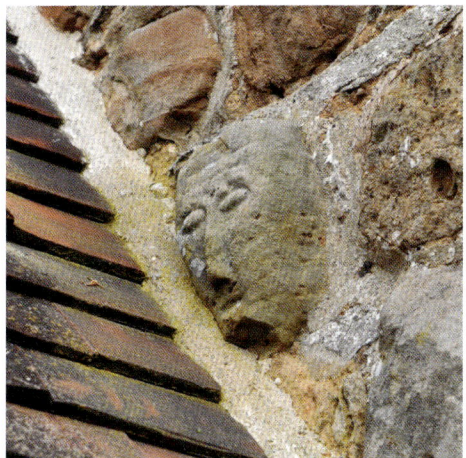

The Celts valued the head above all other parts of the body, believing it to be the seat of the soul and the power-centre of human action, and – along with the tree and the well – a further powerful medium for communication with the OtherWorld.

There are regular examples of places which closely combined well worship with this recognition at least of a belief in the cult of the head. And these convictions did not end with the introduction of Christianity.

In very many christianised sites, there are tales told of saints' heads being struck off (and sometimes, like in the case of St Winifride, being stuck back on again) or, as in Peterchurch and Tremeirchion, of water emerging from the mouths of a saint.

Many Christian shrines still contain skulls, often elaborately encased in silver or gold, and there is a powerful tradition of the representation of holy men and women in portraits and sculptures cradling their own decapitated heads.

opposite and above: offerings left in the great yew
right above: St John the Baptist Church
right middle: one of the two ancient carved stone heads at St John the Baptist Church
right below: St John the Baptist Holy Well directly below the yew

BORDERLANDS

below: the 'Green Man' / St Peter spout in full flow

opposite above: the statue of St Peter, above the porch, St Peter's Church

opposite below: the 'magical' fish in St Peter's Church, Peterchurch

PRE-CHRISTIAN SACRED SPRINGS

the golden valley and the golden chain

St Peter's Well
Peterchurch, Herefordshire
OS Outdoor Leisure Map No.13:
SO 353 388

After leaving St Paul on the 'bwlch' above Hay-on-Wye, legend has it that St Peter followed the Golden Valley to a place that was to become the village of Peterchurch. Here he founded a place of worship and blessed the waters of the well in which he baptised his new converts.

In addition, it is claimed that he caught somewhere a huge fish which emerged from its waters complete with collar and golden chain, which he then deposited in the well. A model of St Peter's magical fish (which appears to be a trout), complete with its chain, can still be seen high up on the wall inside the mediaeval church at Peterchurch.

But this site has much older origins than the strange stories of this itinerant saint, used as it must have been by local people for many centuries prior to his arrival. Indeed, his elaborate efforts to re-brand the Peterchurch sacred waters clearly point to the existence of a powerful alternative earlier story.

Sacred springs were believed to be the entrances to other worlds, many of which had guardians, often in the form of magical fish.

The slippery inhabitant of Bromere Pool in Shropshire, for example, wore a baldric and sword handed to it for safekeeping by local Anglo-Saxon hero, Wild Edric until either Edric himself or a lawful heir came to claim it. And, in the waters of Ffynnon Gybi in north Wales, the sick would seek the services of a resident eel which was said to coil around the legs of the patient to indicate the success or otherwise of the treatment.

At other springs, frogs and serpents (the latter sometimes winged) guarded the waters, and even more strangely, a fly (believed to be immortal) watched over the Scottish well of St Michael in Banffshire, and at Ffynnon Ddigwg in Caernarvonshire "strange creatures resembling hedgehogs without their spikes" were constantly on patrol.

Peterchurch is one of those rare and pleasing places where our ancient well culture is being re-interpreted for a modern age. The new chapter being written by the current villagers here includes the establishment of the Peterchurch Water Supply Friendly Society which pumps from this ancient spring to the local houses, while, on a good day, the Peterchurch well still gushes forth from the mouth of the 'saint', complete with green beard and hair, clearly harking back to the days of the Celts and their cult of the head.

the most dreadful well in wales

Ffynnon Elian

Llanelian, near Colwyn Bay,
Denbighshire
OS Explorer Map OL17: SH 861 769

Not in the mystic Aelian's grove,
Did feather'd songsters sing of love;
But birds of omen harbour'd there,
And fill'd with boding shrieks the air

Charlotte Wardle, from *St Aelian's, or the Cursing Well*, 1814

So-called curse wells have been recorded within the annals of sacred waters since our earliest records. The Romans certainly used their springs as places where they could seek restitution or revenge. They would inscribe a tablet with a 'message' to a deity, naming the malefactor and sometimes asking for a very specific punishment. A tablet found in *Aquae Sulis* in Bath addressed to the god Sulis Minerva reads "Dodimedis has lost two gloves. He asks that the person who has stolen them should lose his mind and eyes in the temple where she appoint"! And, on another occasion, following the theft of a favourite silver ring here, the victim asked that the thief be "accursed in his blood and eyes and every limb, or even have all of his intestines quite eaten away"!

This method of requesting natural justice, restitution or help for any of life's difficulties was also on offer at one well in north Wales. At Ffynnon Elian in the Llanelian parish of Denbighshire, initials were scratched onto slates or stones before being placed in the well, and a request asked of the saint via the medium of the well guardian.

Initially considered to be a site with strong healing properties, Ffynnon Elian was said to have sprung forth to quench the thirst of the obscure St Elian sometime in the sixth century, although it is almost certain that the benefits of its waters would have been recognised well before the christianising of the spring. At the end of the seventeenth century, the Welsh polymath, Edward Lhuyd observed that petitioners were required to pay a groat (a silver coin worth four English pennies) or its equivalent value in bread in order to obtain a cure for a sick child here. He also reported that the well was used by 'Paphistiaid' (Catholics), an indication that although Catholicism had been outlawed since the time of Henry VIII, there were people who continued to ask for help and healing at the old and trusted sources.

Some time in the last quarter of the eighteenth century, however, the reputation of the well was to change from that of a healing pilgrimage destination to a place where people could wish ill upon their neighbours. The Welsh naturalist and antiquarian, **Thomas Pennant** (1726-1798) was the first to publish a description of Ffynnon Elian in which the word 'curse' was recorded:

the well at Saint Aelian… has been in great repute for the cure of all diseases, by means of the intercession of the saint who was first invoked by earnest prayers in the neighbouring church. He was also applied to on less worthy occasions and made the instrument of discovering thieves, and of recovering stolen goods. Some repair to him to imprecate their neighbours and to request the saint to afflict with sudden death, or with some great misfortune, any persons who may have offended them.

(from *A Tour in Wales*, 1778)

Although Pennant clearly acknowledged the dual nature of Ffynnon Elian, he went on to offer a personal anecdote which probably did more than anything else to cement the negative reputation of the site in the popular imagination:

… three years have not elapsed since I was threatened by a fellow (who imagined I had injured him) with the vengeance of St Aelian and a journey to the well to curse me with effect.

opposite: Ffynnon Elian, Llanelian

BORDERLANDS

below and opposite: Ffynnon Elian
far opposite: Jane Beckerman at Ffynnon Elian

From that time onwards, English travel writers were happy to perpetuate the myth and to reduce the site's options to that of a "wickedly malicious well" which "holds still a strong influence over the ignorant mind". (**Wirt Syke**s, *British Goblins*, 1881)

Pedwas Ffowk was for three years afflicted with a complaint which nobody could understand. She was well and yet she was not well: she was sick and yet she was not sick. That is to say, she had no ache or pain, and her appetite was good.

"What do you mean by that?" asked Pedws. "Someone has gone to the woman who keeps the well," answered the wise man, "and put your name on the register, and thrown a pin into the well, together with a pebble with your initials on it."

Some wrote about "the cursing hag", the grove of trees surrounding the well as "dripping with evil", and that "implacable Welshmen would walk 40 miles to curse their neighbours". The following story of one Pedws Ffowk appeared in *The Welsh Fairy Book* (1908) written by **W Jenkyn Thomas**, and is worth quoting in its entirety:

But all the time she became thinner and thinner, until at last she was nothing but skin and bone. She went to doctor after doctor, but they could not find out what was the matter with her. She consulted quacks also, but even they did her no good.

Finally, she went to a wise man. He, after hearing her story, said, "Someone has put you into St. Elian's Well."

"Well, what is the harm of that?" inquired Pedws, who had not heard of the power of the cursing well. You are cursed," was the reply, "and unless the curse is removed, you will pine away and die."

"But what am I to do?" said Pedws, now thoroughly frightened. "You must go to the woman who keeps the well, and pay her to take you out of the well," was the wise man's advice.

PRE-CHRISTIAN SACRED SPRINGS

Pedws lost no time in going to the guardian of the well, who, for a small fee, agreed to examine her register. Sure enough, the name of Pedws Ffowk was there inscribed, and the date of the entry corresponded with the time when she had begun to waste away. On the payment of another and a larger sum of money the priestess of the fountain agreed to take out of the water the stone on which the initials of Pedws Ffowk were scratched.

From that moment flesh began to grow on her bones, and before long her clothes, which had hung upon her like rags upon a scarecrow, were filled out as well as they had ever been. Pedws lived to a good old age, and her greatest trouble was that she never found out which of her best friends had put her into the well.

The travel writers who provided the fragments of sensationalist evidence of this "backward and primitive" people, were, however, not the only enemies of Ffynnon Elian. Methodism arrived here in the latter years of the eighteenth century and, in 1829, outraged members of the congregation destroyed the site, taking every stone away, and very possibly using some of the original well structure to build their own chapel nearby.

Jane Beckerman – on whose land St Elian's Well now sits and who is sensitively restoring this once-important site – explores the context and attraction of the well's dual characteristics to curse and to cure:

Life was hard in Wales from the end of the eighteenth century. The Napoleonic Wars took Welsh men away from their farms and their other occupations; Enclosure Acts took away common land, making life harder for the landless to graze a few animals; and the weather was particularly bad from the end of the eighteenth century until the third decade of the nineteenth …

People must have felt 'cursed' by life, when illness and poverty were so near at hand; and the promise that the 'curse' could be removed, by simply 'taking out' a pebble or slate with an individual's initials on it would have seemed very inviting. There was a cost involved, at a time when money was very scarce, but the ancient power of this well must have been deeply ingrained in the local community and those further afield.

It would not have continued to be used if this had not been the case.

Beckerman (above) offers an intriguing re-interpretation of St Elian's Well as a place for readjusting the balance of life, for finding a small measure of justice in an unjust age, in stark contrast to the more-commonly propagated view of the site as a centre for all things evil.

st tegla's disease

Ffynnon Degla

Llandegla, near Ruthin, Denbighshire
OS Explorer Map No.256: SJ 194 523

In Welsh, epilepsy is sometimes referred to as *Clwyf Tegla* or 'St Tegla's Disease', so it is no surprise that the sacred waters of Ffynnon Degla are famous for curing epilepsy, as well as scrofula (a form of tuberculosis of the lymph glands).

The site is to be found on the north bank of the River Alyn in Llandegla in Denbighshire and, like that at Llanveynoe, its waters emerge into a small chamber from beneath two shading trees.

Tegla's Well was consecrated in the Christian age to the fourth century Welsh hermit princess Degla, although it almost certainly had much deeper roots. Tristan Gray Hulse has argued that "The identity of the Welsh saint Tegla was so far forgotten at Llandegla by the high middle ages that she was apparently identified … with the possibly-apocryphal but certainly far more famous first-century saint Thecla of Iconium".

PRE-CHRISTIAN SACRED SPRINGS

Whatever its origins, an elaborate ritual which mixed pagan and Christian practices was required here in order to ensure an effective cure.

The well had to be visited on a Friday night after sunset when the patient's feet and hands were washed before s/he recited the Lord's Prayer while walking around the well three (in some versions, nine) times, carrying in a basket a cockerel (if male) or a hen (if female). The unfortunate bird would then be pricked with a sharp pin which was thrown into the waters, after which a groat would be paid to the parish clerk. This was followed by three (or nine?) circuits around the church, carrying the bird and again repeating the Lord's Prayer, after which you were to enter the building and place another groat in the poor box. The next stage in your 'treatment' involved lying under the altar using only a bible as your pillow and the communion cloth as your coverlet until daybreak, when you were instructed to place the bird's beak in your mouth and blow, before letting the poor creature go.

You would then put a final piece of silver in the poor box and return home to await the anticipated death of the cock or the hen which would signify the successful transference of the disease from the patient and into the bird:

The parish clerk of Llandegla in 1855 said that an old man of his acquaintance 'remembered quite well seeing the birds staggering about from the effects of the fit' which had been transferred to them.
Wirt Sykes, from *British Goblins*, 1881

This act clearly reflected the ancient pagan practice of 'scapegoating' in which an animal or a person (originally, the king) carries the suffering of the people, the most significant example of which, in Christian times, was Jesus' sacrifice to take on the sins of the world.

The most recent documented success here was in 1813 when the church sexton's son was 'cured' of his epilepsy, although, according to a writer in the *Archaeologia Cambrensis* in 1856, "money was still thrown into St. Tecla's well, by persons desirous of recovering from fits".

opposite far: Ffynnon Degla, Llandegla
opposite: banner from St Tegla's Church, Llandegla

left: images from the interpretative panel telling the story of how to use St Tegla's Well to attract a cure

BORDERLANDS

the living rock

Depplewell
Depple Wood, Moccas,
near Bredwardine, Herefordshire
OS Outdoor Leisure Map No13:
SO 346 434

The presence of sacred springs in the landscape often determined the location of a church, early Christian priests regularly considering it wisest to build upon foundations laid down in previous ages by previous faiths. In the case of St Michael's and All Angels Church at Moccas, however, the spring also provided the actual building materials.

The Depple or Dipple (a contraction of Drip Well, perhaps) has here created over time a huge calcareous dome of solid rock, and it is this that supplied the stones for the nearby church. The spring water at Moccas petrifies the moss to form travertine or 'tufa', which has solidified with age into a great green mound, hidden deep within a dense thicket of trees.

Although I could find no stories associated with the site, petrifying springs like this one are often associated with the sacred, so it is no surprise that the ecclesiastical authorities decided to utilise this 'living rock' with which to build their church.

PRE-CHRISTIAN SACRED SPRINGS

opposite: Depplewell, Moccas

left above: The tufa-stone Parish Church of St Michael's and All Angels at Moccas was built around 1130 upon the site of an early Welsh monastery dedicated to St Dubricius, and laid to waste by the year 600 through an unwelcome combination of Saxon marauders and yellow plague. (OS Outdoor Leisure Map No13: SO 357 433)

left below: Moccas Dip Well

the mother of the world
St Ann's sacred springs and holy wells

... the traditional pagan worship of mother Goddesses at holy wells, the natural interpretation as the well as a secret entrance into the body of the Earth Mother or even as her womb, the belief in the life-giving or procreative powers of water – all combine to instil in people the certainty that the holy well was the source of fertility.

Janet and Colin Bord, from *Earth Rites: Fertility Practices in Pre-Industrial Britain*, 1982

Although christianised to St Ann – the apocryphal mother of the Virgin Mary – these two sacred springs are likely to also have had much earlier origins. Many pagan gods and goddesses were co-opted by the Christian church as saints for their new faith: Demeter, the Greek goddess of festivals became the male warrior saint, Demetrios; Aphrodite became the 'repentant whore' St Aphrodite; the Roman god Mars was transformed into St Martin; and the protector of sailors, the Roman Gemini blended seamlessly into St James, the patron saint of travellers.

New churches were built upon the foundations of pagan temples by the disciples of the new faith, often at sacred crossroads, and sometimes retaining the original pagan circles of stone for their new boundary walls. Phallic carvings were re-chiselled into Christian crosses, and many old festivals, dates and ceremonies continued in the ecclesiastical calendar, little altered. And failing in its initial objective to destroy all pagan holy well sites, the early Christian church soon realised that a more effective strategy would be to rewrite their histories, populated now by a new cast of super-humans.

A belief in a mother goddess with responsibilities for birth and fertility is at the centre of the pantheon of all early civilisations. The following two wells, today dedicated to St Ann, the mother of the mother of god, are thought to have originally been attributed to the variously-named Danu, Annis, Anu, Britannia, Andraste, Modron or Matrona, the Celtic mother goddess of rivers, springs, magic, wisdom … and new beginnings.

PRE-CHRISTIAN SACRED SPRINGS

St Ann's Well
Aconbury, near Hereford,
Herefordshire
OS Explorer Map No.189:
SO 512 334

St Ann's Well near Aconbury in Herefordshire was reputed to cure eye troubles. The most effective remedies here, as was often the case, were offered by the first water drawn from the well after midnight on Twelfth Night. This was 'the cream of the well', said to bubble out of the ground amidst a shroud of blue smoke.

Once an important site where local women competed for the first healing bucketful, today the well is overgrown and neglected as our priorities have shifted far away from those of fundamental importance in the lives of our ancestors.

The Virtuous Well
Trellech, near Monmouth,
Monmouthshire
OS Landranger Map No.162:
SO 503 051

The well with Ann's name at Trellech is also known as 'The Virtuous Well'.

Trellech is a fascinating place, the location of three so-called 'mysteries'. The first of these are three monoliths known today as Harold's Stones, though clearly erected well before King Harold, a political re-dedication like that observed at so many of our holy well sites. Nobody really knows whether these phallic pillars were ceremonial in nature, the location of fertility rites or of cosmic observations ... a true mystery.

The second is the Tump Turret, forty foot high and nearly four hundred feet in circumference. It was once thought to have been the cemetery of King Harold's men, slain in battle, or, alternatively, the burial place of plague victims. It is more likely, however, to be the remains of a motte and bailey castle of the De Clare family, who built a string of Norman keeps in this area.

As the interior has never been explored – there is said to be a curse against anyone who disturbs the mound – it too retains its secret.

opposite far: stained glass window of St Anne and Mary, Chester Cathedral
opposite near: wheat field, near St Ann's Well, Aconbury

left: St Ann's Well, Aconbury (after our clearance)
above: Harold's Stones, Trellech
below: one side of the stone sun-dial in St Nicolas' Church, Trellech, depicting Harold's Stones

The final 'mystery' is the so-called Virtuous Well. Situated in a field on the eastern edge of the village of Trellech beside the Tintern road, it is said to mix water from four separate springs, three of which contain iron, and each offering a cure for a different complaint.

There is a theory that the water which emerges here runs first under Harold's Stones and that the well may originally have been used in Druidical ceremonies. Others have claimed that fairies dance around the well on Midsummer's Eve, and drink its water from harebell cups at sunrise.

A writer in the 1600s claimed that if the waters were drunk in the morning on an empty stomach, they would cure "scurvy, collick and distempers".

Its speciality, however, seems to have been the relief of eye ailments and "complaints peculiar to women"!

left and above: colourful 'clouties' left at The Virtuous Well, Trelleck
above: one of The Viruous Well's resident frogs

opposite: The Virtuous Well

This was and still seems to be an important site for both the pagan and the Christian pilgrim, evidenced by the many strips of cloth and ribbons (or 'clouties') tied onto the overhanging hedgerow, and the offerings of flowers, stones, shells, candles and other objects placed on the ledges and in the niches of this beautifully-elaborate horseshoe-shaped well site.

The 'cloutie' tradition was based upon a belief that if you rubbed the injured part of your body with a cloth soaked in the sacred waters, then hung it on a tree near the well, your complaint would slowly disappear as the fabric naturally rotted away. It is ironic that today, plastic and other non bio-degradable objects are often seen left at this and other well sites!

St Ann's was also an important wishing well. The petitioner would be required to throw a small metal object into the waters and count the number of bubbles that resulted, their rapidity or otherwise determining how quickly their wish would be granted … and, no bubbles at all meant that they had been denied.

On other occasions, young girls anxious to know how long they would have to wait until their wedding day, would drop a pebble into the water, each bubble, it was said, counting as one month.

PRE-CHRISTIAN SACRED SPRINGS

BORDERLANDS

One legend even claimed that nuns used a three-mile-long secret tunnel from Tintern Abbey to take the waters here, unobserved, although history suggests that there were only monks at Tintern.

Another tale tells of a local farmer who foolishly dug up the fairy ring around the well, claiming that he "didn't like all them silly tales". The next day when he went to draw water, he found the well was completely dry, but to him only; all of the other villagers were able to fill their buckets as usual.

The farmer tried to collect his water repeatedly over a number of days, even waiting expectantly behind others who left with full buckets, but as soon as he dipped his pail into the well, the waters receded and he was left with nothing once again.

This went on for many days until, one morning, the farmer met with a little old man who he had never seen before, sitting on the wall of the well. The stranger told him that he had upset the fairies and that he should replace the turf he had removed. This he immediately did and his bucket filled once more with the life-giving waters of the Virtuous Well.

right: The Virtuous Well, Trellech

a modern day 'fairy'
emerging from Havelock Well
Much Wenlock, Shropshire
OS Explorer Map No.217: SO 614 997

CRUELTY AND CULTURE
the fine art of bathing in roman britain

Although Julius Caesar led the first Roman expedition to Britain in 55 BC, it was not until 43 AD – when Claudius landed here with 50,000 well-trained fighting men – that our real engagement with this most organised of empires began. Within five years, Rome had subjugated much of the southern part of Britain.

Many who survived the early onslaught of this brutal military superpower fled west to the heavily-forested hills of Wales where they continued for many decades to offer stubborn resistance to the notion of a Roman province of Britannia.

The first attacks on the area we now know as Wales and its Borderlands were around 47 AD. At this time, the territory was occupied by five tribal groupings: the Deceangli in the north-east; the Ordovices in the north-west and central areas; the Cornovii in the central borderlands; the Demetae in the south-west; and the Silures in the south-east.

left: the main bath house complex at *Isca Augusta* (thanks to Cadw, Welsh Government for permission to photograph)

As Rome's armies pushed west and north across Britain, a long chain of military outposts and towns was built to both wage war upon the local Welsh tribes and then to consolidate their conquests. Ironically, these fortresses were often built on the foundations of existing British hill forts.

By 90 AD, most of the native Welsh population had been suppressed and almost all of what was to become England and Wales had fallen under various levels of Roman rule, with the possible exception of the lands of the Ordovices, significantly omitted on a mosaic map in the Forum in Rome said to show the full extent of the Roman Empire.

The strategy of the Roman invaders was a combination of cruelty and culture, their aim to both conquer and co-opt.

The bath house at these sites of occupation was an ever-present component of this imperial architectural and ideological blueprint, introducing both the sophisticated Roman discipline of cleanliness, at the same time as offering a new panoply of water spirits to add to those already revered by the local people.

BORDERLANDS

where a spring rises

where a spring rises or a river flows, there should we build altars and offer sacrifices

Seneca, Roman first century AD
Stoic philosopher

Religion was closely intertwined with all aspects of life in the Empire and taking a bath in the Roman era was much more than just a chance to wash off the dirt from the day: it was a religious experience, a reconnecting with one of the elemental forces which played such a dominant part in the minds of our ancestors. Washing the body and purifying the spirit were closely linked, separating the civilised from the barbarian.

The most significant of the Roman water sect sites in Britain was that established in 43 AD around the mineral springs of *Aquae Sulis* at Bath in Somerset. The cult of the goddess Sulis Minerva here seems to have been based upon an amalgam of the multi-talented Minerva – the Roman goddess of medicine, poetry, wisdom, commerce, weaving, crafts and magic – and Sulis, the local Celtic deity of the thermal springs.

(A similar cultural syncretism is evident at the much smaller baths and temple complex of Nodens at Lydney, near Chepstow, built at the end of the fourth century AD, explored below.

And in Caerwent, Mars-Ocelus was the result of the coupling of a native Celtic nature god with a leading Roman divinity.)

below: the garden spring at the Roman Water Shrine in Swainshill, Kenchester

opposite: an overflow channel from the Roman sacred spring of *Aquae Sulis*, Bath, Somerset

Most deities found in Roman bath houses had strong association with health: statues of Asclepius, the ancient Greek god of medicine and healing, and his daughters Hygieia (Hygiene), Iaso (Medicine), Aceso (Healing), Aglaea (Healthy Glow) and Panacea (Universal Remedy) were commonplace in bath houses, to ensure the full benefits of the healing waters.

And military bath houses – usually built outside the main fortifications – often called upon the favours of another Roman deity, Fortuna Balnearis (Fortuna of the Baths) for protection, especially when campaigning in remote and dangerous territories like the Welsh Borderlands.

The architectural conventions of the great public Roman *thermae* usually stipulated the provision of a number of rooms of varying temperature: a cold room or *frigidarium* in which to disrobe, as well as to cool down and to take a cold bath at the end of your treatment; a warm room or *tepidarium* in which to acclimatise the body in readiness for the hot room or *calidarium* with its heated floor. And, some establishments included an even hotter room, the sweat chamber or *laconicum*, so named after Laconica, the homeland of the uncompromising Spartans.

At Caerleon near Newport in south Wales, the magnificence of the first century legionary fortress spa facilities is clear to see.

At most of these sites, and in particular those with strong associations with a healing deity, votive offerings were thrown into the waters as remuneration to the appropriate healing or answering god – figurines, tools, weapons or anatomical models of the body parts in question in the hope for or in recognition of a miracle cure. And curses could also be laid.

BORDERLANDS

BATHING IN ROMAN BRITAIN

the 'Old Work' archway, - the largest free-standing Roman ruin in England - leading to the baths, *Viroconium Cornoviorum*, Wroxeter, Shropshire

the ghost of a dead city

Viroconium Cornoviorum
Wroxeter, near Shrewsbury, Shropshire
OS Explorer Map No.241:
SJ 565 087

To-day the Roman and his trouble
Are ashes under Uricon.

AE Housman (1859-1936)
from his poem 'On Wenlock Edge the wood's in trouble' (*A Shropshire Lad*, 1896)

At its peak, *Viroconium Cornoviorum* – at present-day Wroxeter some five miles south-east of Shrewsbury – was thought to have been the fourth largest city in Roman Britain, a substantial site equal in size to Pompeii.

Initially established in 58 AD, it was an important military fortress from which to attack the Welsh, large enough to accommodate an entire legion of 5,500 men. From about 88 AD, however, *Viroconium* became a civilian settlement when the soldiers appear to have left, after which time, the city thrived for perhaps another 600 years, with an estimated population at its height of up to 15,000.

53

BORDERLANDS

The suffix, *Cornoviorum* means 'of the Cornovii', the local tribe whose self-governing capital (or *civitas*) it became, suggesting the Cornovii's incorporation into the empire (as we shall see also happened at *Venta Silurum* with the Silures). With the reduction of the likelihood of attack, the troops were, it seems, no longer needed here for protection.

Though much still remains unexplored below ground at this site, the most impressive features currently visible are the luxurious second century AD municipal baths (completed around the year 150), and the remains of what is now known as the 'Old Work'. This huge wall is the largest free-standing Roman structure in England, dividing the baths from the exercise hall in the heart of what once was the city, both, according to some authorities, erected on the instigation of the Emperor Hadrian.

The ruins of *Viroconium* became one of the first archaeological visitor attractions in Britain, and many writers drew inspiration from the messages they were able to read within its crumbling walls. **Wilfred Owen** (1893-1918) attended archaeological digs at Viroconium, and wrote 'Uriconium: an Ode' in 1913:

left: three views of the remains of the great bath house and exercise hall at *Viroconium*, showing the elaborate system of under-floor heating

opposite: The shallow, open-air plunge pool in the exercise yard at *Viroconium Cornoviorum* was used to close the pores at the end of a hot bathing session.

BORDERLANDS

Uriconium: an Ode

It lieth low near merry England's heart
Like a long-buried sin; and Englishmen
Forget that in its death their sires had part.
And, like a sin, Time lays it bare again
To tell of races wronged,
And ancient glories suddenly overcast,
And treasures flung to fire and rabble wrath.
If thou hast ever longed
To lift the gloomy curtain of Time Past,
And spy the secret things that Hades hath,
Here through this riven ground take such a view.
The dust, that fell unnoted as a dew,
Wrapped the dead city's face like mummy-cloth:
All is as was: except for worm and moth.

Since Jove was worshipped under Wrekin's shade
Or Latin phrase was writ in Shropshire stone,
Since Druid chants desponded in this glade
Or Tuscan general called that field his own,
How long ago? How long?
How long since wanderers in the Stretton Hills
Met men of shaggy hair and savage jaw,
With flint and copper prong,
Aiming behind their dikes and thorny grilles?
Ah! those were days before the axe and saw,
Then were the nights when this mid-forest town
Held breath to hear the wolves come yelping down,
And ponderous bears 'long Severn lifted paw,
And nuzzling boars ran grunting through the shaw.

Ah me! full fifteen hundred times the wheat
Hath risen, and bowed, and fallen to human hunger
Since those imperial days were made complete.
The weary moon hath waxen old and younger
These eighteen thousand times
Without a shrine to greet her gentle ray.
And other temples rose; to Power and Pelf,
And chimed centurial chimes
Until their very bells are worn away.
While King by King lay cold on vaulted shelf
And wars closed wars, and many a Marmion fell,
And dearths and plagues holp sire and son to hell;
And old age stiffened many a lively elf
And many a poet's heart outdrained itself.

I had forgot that so remote an age
Beyond the horizon of our little sight,
Is far from us by no more spanless gauge
Than day and night, succeeding day and night,
Until I looked on Thee,
Thou ghost of a dead city, or its husk!
But even as we could walk by field and hedge
Hence to the distant sea
So, by the rote of common dawn and dusk,
We travel back to history's utmost edge.
Yea, when through thy old streets I took my way,
And recked a thousand years as yesterday,
Methought sage fancy wrought a sacrilege
To steal for me such godly privilege!

For here lie remnants from a banquet table –
Oysters and marrow-bones, and seeds of grape –
The statement of whose age must sound a fable;
And Samian jars, whose sheen and flawless shape
Look fresh from potter's mould.
Plasters with Roman finger-marks impressed;
Bracelets that from the warm Italian arm
Might seem to be scarce cold;
And spears – the same that pushed the Cymry west –
Unblunted yet; with tools of forge and farm
Abandoned, as a man in sudden fear
Drops what he holds to help his swift career:
For sudden was Rome's flight, and wild the alarm.
The Saxon shock was like Vesuvius' qualm.

O ye who prate of modern art and craft.
Mark well that Gaulish brooch, and test that screw!
Art's fairest buds on antique stem are graft.

BATHING IN ROMAN BRITAIN

Under the sun is nothing wholly new!
At Viricon today
The village anvil rests on Roman base
And in a garden, may be seen a bower
With pillars for its stay
That anciently in basilic had place.
The church's font is but a pagan dower:
A Temple's column, hollowed into this.
So is the glory of our artifice,
Our pleasure and our worship, but the flower
Of Roman custom and of Roman power.

O ye who laugh and, living as if Time
Meant but the twelve hours ticking round your dial,
Find it too short for thee, watch the sublime,
Slow, epochal time-registers awhile,
Which are Antiquities.
O ye who weep and call all your life too long
And moan: Was ever sorrow like to mine?
Muse on the memories
That sad sepulchral stones and ruins prolong.
Here might men drink of wonder like strong wine
And feel ephemeral troubles soothed and curbed.
Yet farmers, wroth to have their laws disturbed,
Are sooner roused for little loss to pine
Than we are moved by mighty woes long syne.

Above this reverend ground, what traveller checks?
Yet cities such as these one time would breed
Apocalyptic visions of world-wrecks.
Let Saxon men return to them, and heed!
They slew and burnt,
But after, prized what Rome had given away
Out of her strength and her prosperity.
Have they yet learnt
The precious truth distilled from Rome's decay?
Ruins! On England's heart press heavily!
For Rome hath left us more than walls and words
And better yet shall leave; and more than herds
Or land or gold gave the Celts to us in fee;
E'en Blood, which makes poets sing and prophets see.

above: Roman masonry evident in the walls of St Andrew's Church, Wroxeter
below: "The church's font is but a pagan dower" (Wilfred Owen), St Andrew's Church

In her poem 'Viroconium', the Shropshire novelist and poet, **Mary Webb** (1881-1927) also heard the spirit here of

"A shrineless god whose songs abide / Forever in the countryside":

The pillars stand, with alien grace,
In churches of a younger race;
The chiselled column, black and rough,
Becomes a roadside cattle-trough:

The skulls of men who, right or wrong,
Still wore the splendour of the strong,
Are shepherds' lanterns now, and shield
Their candles in the lambing field.

above: St Andrew's Church, Kenchester

opposite: the Roman villa reconstructed in 2010 as part of the Channel 4 TV series *Rome Wasn't Built in a Day*

BATHING IN ROMAN BRITAIN

BORDERLANDS

rome's state-of-the-art leisure centre in wales

Isca Augusta
Caerleon, Monmouthshire
OS Explorer Map No.152: SO 340 906

On the river Usk at Caerleon, a little way north-east of Newport, is the only still visible legionary barracks (or *castra*) in Europe, the headquarters of the Second Augustan Legion between 74 and 300 AD. The name Caerleon came from the Welsh for 'fortress of the legion', although the Romans called it *Isca*, based upon 'Wysg', the Welsh name for the river, Usk.

The *Isca Augusta* site is world famous for its amphitheatre (thought in the past to have been the 'Round Table' of King Arthur), its huge fortress baths (even larger than those of *Aquae Sulis*) and its extensive military barracks, as well as the recently discovered remains of a major Roman harbour on the River Usk.

left and above: the main bath house complex at *Isca Augusta*
(thanks to Cadw, Welsh Government for permission)

opposite above: the amphitheatre, Caerleon
(thanks to Cadw, Welsh Government for permission)
opposite centre: the remains of the small bath house thought to have been for the use of the gladiators, situated next to the amphitheatre at Caerleon
opposite right: armour store,
National Roman Legion Museum, Caerleon
(thanks to National Museum Wales)

BATHING IN ROMAN BRITAIN

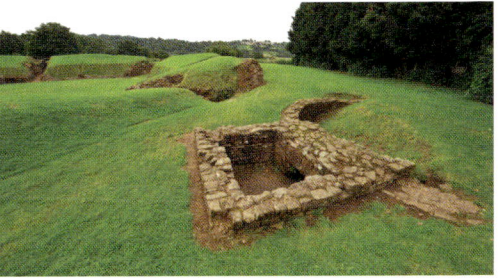
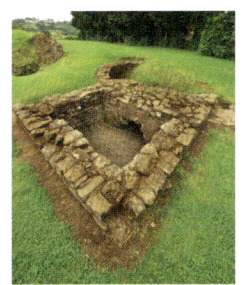

BORDERLANDS

below: the main bath house complex at *Isca Augusta*
(thanks to Cadw, Welsh Government for permission to photograph)

opposite: the remains of Lydney Park Roman Baths
(with the kind permission of Lord Bledisloe of the Lydney Park Estate)

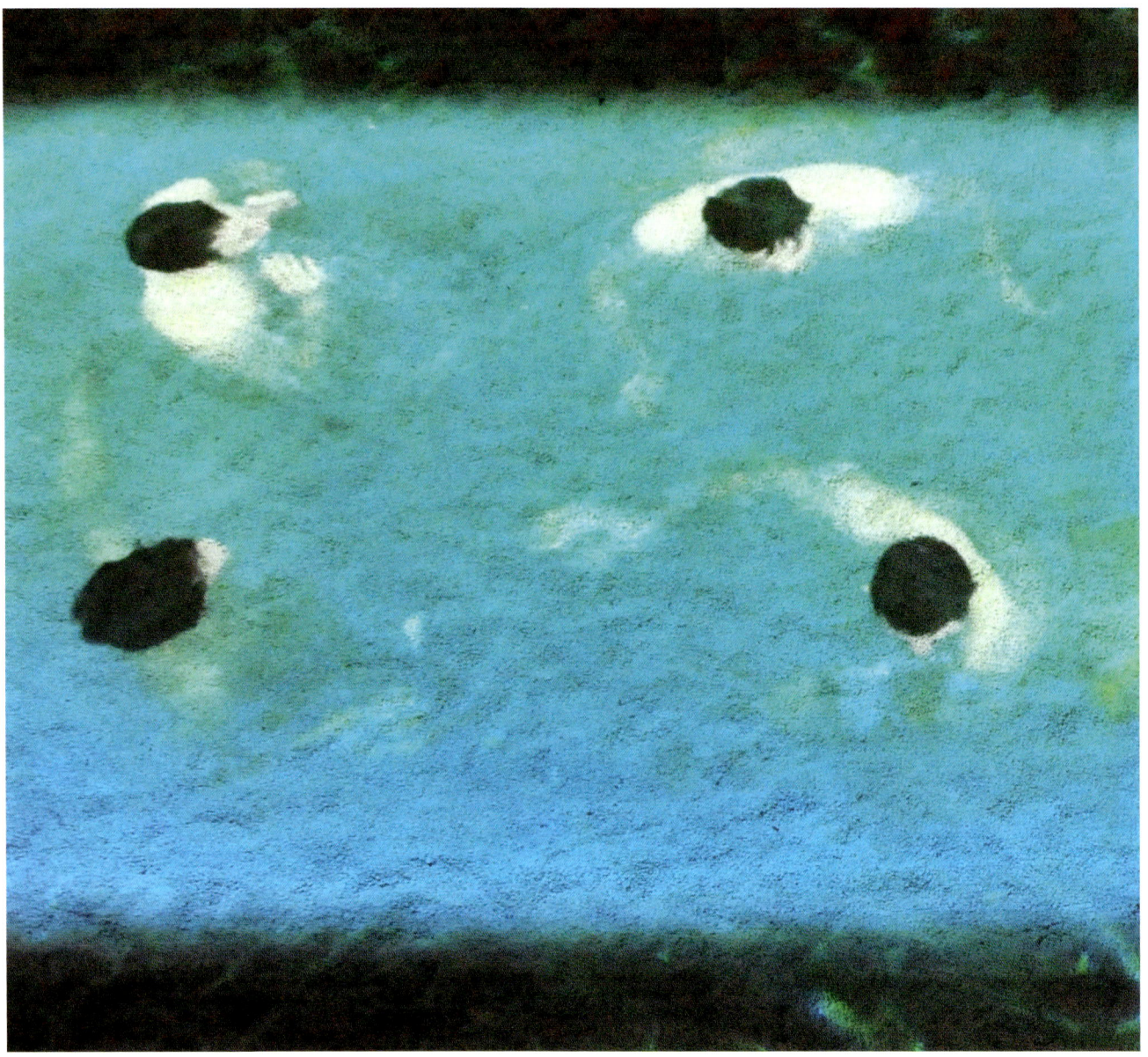

who was nodens?

Lydney Park Roman Temple and Bath

Dwarf Hill, Lydney, Forest of Dean, Gloucestershire
OS Explorer Map.OL14: SO 614 027

Situated on Dwarf Hill between Gloucester and Chepstow in the Forest of Dean, and said to have been dedicated to Nodens, a little-known deity, the evocative ruins of the Roman temple and baths complex at Lydney Park are now part of the large country estate of the Bledisloe family.

There are a number of theories as to who Nodens was. Some say he might have been a Roman god of healing, evidenced here by the large number of cult objects and votive offerings found, including 320 pins, 300 bracelets, thousands of coins, nine statuettes of dogs in stone or bronze, an oculist's stamp, tablets referring to cures, as well as some used for cursing.

The most impressive of these objects is a fine bronze greyhound: in Classical times, dogs were associated with healing and sacred dogs were regularly found in Greek and Roman temples, there, it seems, to lick the infected parts of the sufferer's body!

An alternative explanation was proffered by the author of *The Lord of the Rings*, JRR Tolkien, who was himself a member of the 1920s Lydney Park excavation team led by Sir Mortimer Wheeler.

Tolkien believed that Nodens might have been the early Celtic Irish god, 'Nodens the Catcher', who survived in Irish legend as Nuada, and in Wales as Llud Llaw Ereint, the original King Lear.

Whatever the explanation, the Lydney site, it seems, was an important healing shrine, at which the bath complex played a significant part.

BORDERLANDS

building on the stones of the past

Venta Silurum
Caerwent, Monmouthshire
OS Explorer Map No.152: SO 470 907

Venta … whose name neither the rage of men nor time has yet extinguished.

William Camden, antiquarian, writing in 1586

right: the village launderette built on the site of *Venta Silurum*'s bath house

opposite:
the remains of the Romano-Celtic temple at *Venta Silurum*, Caerwent

The pacification of the Silures in south-east Wales took more than twenty-five years of bloody military endeavour against fierce local resistance.

Following their surrender in 74/75 AD, however, the Roman victors built an impressive walled city here, at a place we now know as Caerwent.

By the year 200, *Venta Silurum* – or the 'market of the Silures' – had become the largest Roman civilian settlement in Wales, and the administrative capital of the tribe, who had been granted a form of local government, a partial devolution a little perhaps like Wales' relationship with the British state for most of its modern life.

Caerwent today illustrates better than anywhere else the way in which civilizations have built, layer upon layer, upon the constructions of their predecessors.

When the Romans who had themselves built upon Silurian foundations left, the settlement fell into decay until it became the site of a monastery built by the Irish Saint Tathan, then later that of a small Norman castle.

And, even today, we continue to build upon the stones of the past as the modern-day launderette in Caerwent sits, appropriately perhaps, on top of the site of the original Roman bath house, here.

Caerwent is now a sleepy hamlet which has little to suggest its deep layers of history as you drive through it on the A48 from Newport to Chepstow. Stop and take a walk to both sides of the road, however, and you are transported back millennia, by the evocative stones that remain, in the best preserved Roman walls in Britain.

BORDERLANDS

above and opposite: the impressive Roman walls and watch towers at *Venta Silurum*

BORDERLANDS

love and war

Balineae Silures

Castell Collen, near Llandrindod Wells,
Radnorshire / Powys
OS Explorer Map No.200: SO 628 055

The little-known Roman fort of Castell Collen, a mile or so north-west of Llandrindod Wells, sits on the crest of a knoll overlooking a horseshoe bend in the river Ithon.

It was the site of eighteen training camps founded in the Flavian period by Julius Frontinus in his campaign to subdue the Silures, and is the most significant example of Roman defences in central Wales.

above right: Roman soldier at *Viroconium Cornoviorum* (Wroxeter), near Shrewsbury
right: model of *Balineae Silures* (used courtesy of Radnorshire Museum, Llandrindod Wells)

opposite: *Balineae Silures*, near Llandrindod Wells

BORDERLANDS

Given the scale of the site and the number of soldiers it was catering for, it is not surprising to find that Castell Collen had an extensive bath house complex – known as *Balineae Silures*, in recognition of the local Celtic tribe.

As the power of the Roman empire faded, Castell Collen was abandoned (in around 400 AD) and over the years the site, like so many others, was raided for stone for local buildings, leaving little above ground level today to suggest the scale and importance of this once formidable military base.

Excavated in 1911, then again more extensively between 1954 and 1956, one of the most intriguing items found here was a silver ring with the crudely-inscribed message 'AMOR DVLCIS' meaning 'sweet love'.

right above: the barely visible outline of Castell Collen Romano-British fort
right middle and below: what little remains of *Balineae Silures*, the large military bath house at Castell Collen built outside of the walls of the fortress

lost and found

Prestatyn Roman Bath House

Melyd Avenue, Prestatyn, Denbighshire
OS Explorer Map No.265: SJ 064 817

Only discovered in 1934, the small Roman bath house at Prestatyn – which is all that remains of what may be the lost Roman settlement of *Varae* and currently sits in the middle of a sprawling housing estate – was built around 120 AD and extended thirty years later.

Prestatyn Roman Bath House, Denbighshire

It was probably constructed by and for the soldiers of the Twentieth Legion based in *Castra Deva Victrix* (modern day Chester, some twenty miles to the south-east) who were involved in mining lead here and its shipping from the nearby harbour.

It comprises of the usual cold and hot rooms, as well as a steam room and an icy, invigorating plunge pool fed by a local spring by means of a timber aqueduct.

BORDERLANDS

the water nymphs of the wye

New Weir Roman Villa and Water Shrine

Weir Gardens, Swainshill, Herefordshire
OS Explorer Map No.202: SO 437 418

The New Weir Roman site occupies an idyllic setting in the Weir Gardens, near Swainshill in Herefordshire, above the north bank of the River Wye. It lies about half a mile south of the Romano-British walled-town of Kenchester, and a quarter of a mile west of the Roman road leading south to the fort at Abergavenny and the legionary fortresses at Usk and Caerleon. It is currently managed by the National Trust.

In 1891, an impressive and unusual octagonal stone cistern was uncovered here, and later, in 1977, two large stone buttresses beside the river and many large dressed stones in its waters which probably acted as landing stages for Roman nobility were recorded. Experts believe that these finds – alongside the extensive terraced gardens – point to this being the important site of a high-status Roman villa of the third or fourth century AD and its elaborate Romano-Celtic shrine (or *nymphaeum*) devoted to the water nymphs which were thought to inhabit the Wye.

BATHING IN ROMAN BRITAIN

no second bath

he who has bathed in Christ has no need of a second bath!

the words of the fourth century ascetic, **Saint Jerome**

When the Romans eventually left in the early years of the fifth century – after the Visigoths had sacked Rome in 410 AD – bath house culture declined in Britain, and with it the adherence to Roman deities. Tensions were increased in the dark years that followed by political strife and instability, and wave upon wave of new, less-sophisticated invaders.

And in its earliest days, the new Christian faith frowned upon those who continued to take recreational baths for pleasure; some even believing that the devil resided in thermal waters:

Bathing is not absolutely forbidden ... If you are ill you need it; so it is not a sin. If a man is healthy, it cossets and relaxes the body and conduces to lust.

Barsanuphius of Gaza,
sixth century Palestinian hermit who is said to have lived in absolute seclusion for fifty years

Bathing now, in the eyes of those that espoused the new faith, only became acceptable as long as it wasn't enjoyable. There are many tales told of early Christian ascetics spending large parts of their lives in freezing waters.

The Cornish saints Neot and Petroc regularly immersed themselves in wells for the sake of their souls. And St Anthony – who was thought of as 'the father of monasticism' – had an isolated forest well with the coldest of all waters to prove it.

But, if you were unwilling to brave the freezing waters for your god, then being dirty was the next best thing, as an alternative spiritual triumph over the body. Much later, even 'science' suggested that a layer of dirt on the skin would protect against infection and disease.

This admonition not to over-emphasise the cleanliness of the body to the detriment of the soul – antithetical to Roman bath house thinking – was clearly understood as, more than ten centuries later, Queen Elizabeth I (1533-1603) is reported to have claimed that she took a bath once a month, "whether she needed to or not"!

opposite: the intriguing octagonal Roman water cistern at New Weir Roman Water Shrine in Swainshill, Kenchester

above: one of the river buttresses on the Wye at Swainshill

opposite: Chester Cathedral was the resting place and shrine of St Werburgh from the tenth century until its desecration in 1538, and the parish church of St Oswald until 1881

* MOVING WATERS AT THEIR PRIEST-LIKE TASK
holy wells in the age of the saints

Christianity spread across Britain from the third century onwards, its earliest records here being of martyrdoms.

The saints Aaron and Julius – who appear to have been soldiers of the Second Augustan Legion based at Caerleon – both perished at the hands of the Romans, before Constantine the Great pronounced Christianity the official religion of the Empire in 313 AD.

Ascetic ideas from saints like Antony of Egypt – who lived for forty years as a hermit in the desert – encouraged the establishment of new monastic settlements.

Here worldly comforts were exchanged for little sleep, basic food, an abstinence from encounters with the opposite sex and hard manual labour, in an effort to achieve union with god, although the Welsh emphasis seems to have been for more of a communal monasticism rather than a hermetic life, where there is even evidence of some clergy being allowed to marry.

* John Keats (1795-1821), from his *Last Sonnet*, 1820

A major controversy raged during the early centuries of the new faith concerning the deep layers of belief upon which the developing Celtic-British Church was based. Pelagius, a fifth century British monk argued for a more humanistic and egalitarian interpretation against Rome's insistence on 'original sin' and a pampered and hierarchical clergy:

Abolish the rich and you will have no more poor ...

the words of the 'Sicilian Briton',
a follower of Pelagianism,
writing in the early fifth century

It is easy to see how these views would have been attractive here, particularly on the Celtic side of the border with its roots in native paganism and so often oppressed by the inappropriate ideas of the next wave of invaders.

Other liturgical variations between the British and Roman Churches included the relative authorities of the disciples John and Peter; their differing head-shaving practices, those of the British considered a throw-back to druidic times by Rome; the observance of the 'sabbath' on Saturday in Britain, rather than Sunday as was favoured by Rome; the British Church's emphasis on the cult of saints; and, most significantly, the dating of Easter.

HOLY WELLS IN THE AGE OF THE SAINTS

As for our sacred springs, the new Christian missionaries were initially instructed to destroy the pagan sites, along with all other reminders of the 'hydrolatrous' beliefs they supported.

It was at this time that the predominantly female nature of the well spirit was made masculine; the druid and the bard became the monk and the priest; and pagan magical springs became Christian holy wells.

Such were the sites' strength within the popular imagination, however, that this was rarely fully achieved, and an alternative strategy had to be adopted of 'converting' the pagan sites and their ceremonies to a new Christian usage.

As Francis Jones, the great authority on the holy wells of Wales wrote in 1954: "the older deities of well, hill and megalith survived in a new guise", as the new faith and the ancient beliefs developed in parallel in an often-uncomfortable dialogue.

Churches were built over sacred springs and Christian saints replaced pagan deities as the spiritual benefactor, often at the places where a severed head fell. In addition, new Christian well sites were developed, often associated with a saint's visit, a miracle or martyrdom.

The rich red stain of iron found in chalybeate wells provided evidence for believers of a saint's violent death – and a deeper reference all the way back to Christ's suffering – at the same time as reminding them of the well's original occupant, the female Earth Spirit and her responsibility for procreation and birth.

The story of the sacred waters in this period became one of definitions and acknowledgements: the healing properties of the well remained, but praise was now due for its services to a new religious master or mistress. The red water in chalybeate wells now became Christ's or one of his saint's blood, instead of that of the menstruating goddess.

springing freshly amidst decay *

holy wells of St Mary

Mary is thought to have been a Jewish woman from Nazareth in Galilee. Although her parents were said to be the elderly couple, St Joachim and St Anne, Mary's betrothal to Joseph would have taken place when she was only twelve years of age (in keeping with Jewish custom), and her 'virgin birth' of Jesus – 'by the divine intervention of the Holy Spirit' – just a year later.

Recognised in both Christian and Islamic faiths, Marian beliefs are held most strongly within the Catholic and Orthodox churches. It was said that, upon Mary's death (possibly in the year 41 AD), she was assumed to heaven.

Some believe that wells once the preserve of pagan goddesses were, under Christianity, extensively re-dedicated to the Virgin Mary. Given her importance within Christian belief – and possibly in this other guise centuries before the Christ story – it is not surprising, then, to find that there are today many wells dedicated to Mary or Our Lady throughout the Borderlands, as elsewhere.

* Felicia Hemans (1793-1835) from her poem *Ffynnon Fair / Our Lady's Well*

and did those feet?

Our Lady Well
Hempsted, near Gloucester, Gloucestershire
OS Landranger Map No.162:
SO 814 173

The impressive fourteenth century well-house at Hempsted, situated in an elevated position in the middle of a sloping field and overlooking the river Severn may once have been dedicated to Ann, Mary's saintly mother. Indeed, some local people still refer to the sacred spring here as St Ann's Well, believing that the well-worn bas-relief carvings in the gable of the eastern wall are those of the draped figure of St Ann, flanked by her daughter St Mary and an angel (or alternatively, her husband).

But some have suggested an even deeper derivation from the similar-sounding 'Wan', the pagan god Woden. Another suggestion is that the carving is a recycled Roman votive tablet to Diana the Huntress; and yet another that it represents the goddess Bridgid (or Coventina), the latter claim lent credence by the age of the sculpture and the fact that her most usual depiction is in triad form, as found at the Roman site in Bath.

above: Our Lady Well, Hempstead, Gloucestershire

opposite: the chalybeate spring, Rock Park, Llandrindod Wells

BORDERLANDS

top: Our Lady Well, Hempstead
bottom: the well-worn bas-relief carving at Our Lady Well

top: Mary's Well house roof, Bodrhyddan Hall
middle: the bathing pool, Mary's Well
below: sitting area inside Mary's Well house

it *will* be a stylish wedding …

Mary's Well
Bodrhyddan Hall, near Rhuddlan, Denbighshire
OS Explorer Map No.264: SJ 048 788

According to the carved letters on one of the outside walls of the octagonal well house at Bodryddan Hall, near Rhuddlan, this was the 1612 work of the famous architect, Inigo Jones.

The impressive chamber with its arched entrance with cherub, iron gate and stone seats is topped by a carved pelican (part of the coat of arms of the estate owners, the Langford family), and sits beside a large rectangular-walled bath.

Dedicated to St Mary, the well is reputed to have had healing properties and been the site of "clandestine weddings", although no accounts of this practice seem to have survived. This may be partly due to the fact that the estate records were destroyed by fire, or, more cynically, that the Grade One Listed Building is today describing itself as "one of the most stylish wedding reception venues in North Wales"!

A more orthodox reading of the work, however, suggests it is of the Virgin herself, addressing a crowd. Long venerated as a place of pilgrimage, one tradition claims that Mary actually visited Hempsted and that the spring here arose at this very spot to quench her thirst.

left: Mary's Well, Bodrhyddan Hall, near Rhuddlan, Denbighshire
above: stained glass window of St Mary from St Michael and All Angels Church, Moccas
below: the cherub guard at Mary's Well-house

BORDERLANDS

right: **Ffynnon Fair,** or **Mary's Well** (OS Landranger Map No. 125: SJ 104 064), situated on the slope between St Mary's Church in Llanfair Caereinion (Montgomery / Powys) and the river Banw below, famous for its relief of arthritis and skin problems, as well, most interestingly, for its ability to protect people from being bewitched

above: the stained glass Annunciation window at Llanfair Caereinion, showing the angel Gabriel giving Mary the news that she has been chosen to carry the Christ child, above images of Ffynnon Fair and St Mary's Church

HOLY WELLS IN THE AGE OF THE SAINTS

Ffynnon Fair, Llanfair Caereinion

BORDERLANDS

fount of the virgin's ruined shrine! *

Ffynnon Fair

Trefnant, near St Asaph, Denbighshire
OS Landranger Map No.116:
SJ 031 709

The Elwy here takes another direction, running west, and then north, along most romantic dingles, varied with meadows, woods, and cavernous rocks: neither is it destitute of antiquities. Y ffynnon fair, or our lady's well, a fine spring, enclosed in an angular wall, formerly roofed; and the ruins of a cross-shaped chapel, finely overgrown with ivy, exhibit a venerable view, in a deep-wooded bottom ... in days of pilgrimage, the frequent haunt of devotees.

Thomas Pennant writing in his
Tour of Wales, 1778 and 1781

St Winifride's Well at Holywell and Ffynnon Fair near Trefnant in Denbighshire were linked by a popular pilgrimage route, as, intriguingly, are the fine designs of their basins. The earliest part of the now-roofless chapel building is thought to date from the thirteenth century, with the chancel being added and the fine polygonal well pool of hewn stone rebuilt in the fifteenth.

Following the Reformation, the well began to fall into disrepair and, by the eighteenth century, the chapel was in ruins and pilgrimages had ceased, although it did continue to build upon its reputation, like that of Bodrhyddan, for secret weddings, becoming known by some as 'the Gretna Green of North Wales'.

Today, only the ivy-clad stones returning to nature, and the constant chatter of the spring waters are left to testify to its long history of worship and of love.

above and opposite:
modern day pilgrims at Ffynnon Fair

The poet **Felicia Hemans** (1793-1835) lived as a child at Rhyllon near St Asaph and would have regularly visited the site.

Here is her poem, entitled 'Ffynnon Fair':

FOUNT of the woods! thou art hid no more
From heaven's clear eye, as in time of yore.
For the roof hath sunk from thy mossy walls,
And the sun's free glance on thy slumber falls;
And the dim tree-shadows across thee pass,
As the boughs are swayed o'er thy silvery glass;
And the reddening leaves to thy breast are blown,
When the autumn wind hath a stormy tone;
And thy bubbles rise to the flashing rain –
Bright Fount! thou art nature's own again!

Fount of the vale! thou art sought no more
By the pilgrim's foot, as in time of yore,
When he came from afar, his beads to tell,
And to chant his hymn at Our Lady's Well.
There is heard no Ave through thy bowers,
Thou art gleaming lone midst thy water flowers!
But the herd may drink from thy gushing wave,
And there may the reaper his forehead lave,
And the woodman seeks thee not in vain –
Bright Fount! thou art nature's own again!

Fount of the Virgin's ruined shrine! *
A voice that speaks of the past is thine!
It mingles the tone of a thoughtful sigh
With the notes that ring through the laughing sky;
Midst the mirthful song of the summer bird,
And the sound of the breeze, it will yet be heard! –
Why is it that thus we may gaze on thee,
To the brilliant sunshine sparkling free?
'Tis that all on earth is of Time's domain –
He hath made thee nature's own again!

Fount of the chapel with ages gray!
Thou art springing freshly amidst decay;
Thy rites are closed, and thy cross lies low,
And the changeful hours breathe o'er thee now.
Yet if at thine altar one holy thought
In man's deep spirit of old hath wrought;
If peace to the mourner hath here been given,
Or prayer from a chastened heart to heaven –
Be the spot still hallowed while Time shall reign,
Who hath made thee nature's own again!

opposite and right:
Ffynnon Fair, Trefnant

man and beast

St Anthony's Well
Edgehills Plantation, near Cinderford,
Forest of Dean, Gloucestershire
OS Explorer Map OL14: SO 670 157

The extremely cold waters here fall from a high stone well-house into a large bathing pool, and on downstream to a larger pool next to the road. Perched on a steep slope in the trees, set deep within the Forest of Dean, this is a most appropriate site to be named after this early Egyptian hermit monk, the patron saint of gravediggers (not to be confused with St Anthony of Padua, the patron of the poor, lost things and barren women). This Anthony, who sought solitude in wildernesses – following Jesus' forty day example – is thought to have been the father of monasticism and the first Christian missionary to Wales, living so it is claimed to the splendid age of 105 (251-356).

This was an immersion well that specialised in the cure of skin complaints, its efficacy later championed by the Cistercian monks of nearby Flaxley Abbey (now a private residence). It was also believed to relieve dogs of the mange, an unusual inclusion as most wells were said to loose their human healing powers if an animal was even sprinkled with their holy waters, let alone immersed within it.

St Anthony's Well,
Forest of Dean

the bride of christ

St Julian(a)'s Well
Ludlow, Shropshire
OS Landranger Map No.137:
SO 518 751

This incongruously-situated well, known locally as St Julian's, was – like St Julian's Church in Shrewsbury – originally dedicated to St Juliana, the female virgin martyr of Nicomedia (in Izmir, Turkey), then under Roman rule.

A convert to Christianity at a dangerous time, Juliana is said to have been imprisoned, tortured and finally beheaded in the year 304 for her refusal to marry a pagan suitor, Eleusius the all-powerful governor of Nicomedia. Seeing herself as already a 'bride of Christ', Juliana preferred death to a pagan husband, telling him: "it is impossible for our bodies to be unified if our hearts militate"!

On my first visit to St Anthony's Well, a dog sprang from the forest and into the well; on the second occasion, a man was seeking relief from a painful eczema, suggesting a continuation of the importance of the site for both human and canine sufferers, and a willingness to perpetuate the painful embrace of ascetic necessities in the search for a miracle cure.

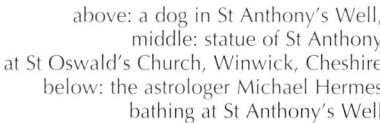

above: a dog in St Anthony's Well,
middle: statue of St Anthony
at St Oswald's Church, Winwick, Cheshire
below: the astrologer Michael Hermes
bathing at St Anthony's Well

While in prison, her suitor became her judge … and her torturer. Stripped naked, she was flogged, hung by the hair and her face burned with a heated iron to erase her beauty. It is also said that she was tempted by a demon, masquerading as an angel, who she managed through prayer to overcome. It was claimed that her tears quenched the fire prepared to burn her, and she emerged unhurt from a boiling caldron of lead, before her eventual decapitation at the age of eighteen. Eleusius, so the story goes, was later eaten by a lion when shipwrecked on a deserted island.

Saint Juliana, the patron saint of healing waters, has traditionally offered protection from fever and all contagious diseases, as well as being invoked, rather ironically given her story, for the safe delivery of women in labour!

Today, St Julian / Juliana's Well is situated on a traffic island at the junction of Livesey Road and St Julian's Avenue in Ludlow, propped up against a large chestnut tree. Only its roof is still visible above the ground, although a neighbour of the well, Miss Paddy Willis kindly showed me photographs of the chamber when it was fully excavated last in November 1994.

St Julian / Juliana's Well, Ludlow

BORDERLANDS

below: St Julian / Juliana's Well, Ludlow
opposite: St Dubricius' holy well
opposite near: stained glass window at St Dubricius' Church, Hentland: the hedgehog at the saint's feet (an 'erchin' in the local Celtic dialect) was the symbol of Erchinfield, as Hentland was once known.

born of water and of fire

Holy Well of St Dubricius

Hentland, near Ross-on-Wye,
Herefordshire
OS Explorer Map No.189: OS 544 264

Hên-llan, the Welsh language origin of Hentland, means 'old church-enclosure'. This was the site of an important early Welsh monastery, built in the sixth century by Saint Dubricius (or 'Dyfig' in Welsh, 'Devereux' in Norman French). Here (and at his second monastery at Moccas), he instructed many of Wales' best-known holy men, including St Teilo and St Samson.

Over a period of just seven years, more than two thousand clergy are said to have passed through his ecclesiastical establishments before being sent out to spread the word. Dubricius himself also travelled widely, was in regular contact with the Saints Illtyd and Cadog, and was so eminent that he was even said to have officiated at the crowning of King Arthur at Caer Fudi (thought to have been either Silchester or Woodchester) in 513!

Dubricius was amongst the most important of early Welsh saints, born most likely in Chilstone in the parish of Madley near Hereford, the illegitimate son of Efrddyl, the daughter of King Peibio Clafrog.

The legend of the saint's birth is well worth repeating. It was said that his grandfather tied Dubricius' mother in a sack and threw her into the river Wye when he discovered that she was pregnant. Continually washed up on the shore, the king undeterred then built a funeral pyre and threw his daughter onto it alive and set it alight.

Saved from the waters and the fire, Dubricius and Efrddyl were both eventually reconciled with Peibio when the baby saint – born like a phoenix rising out of the flames – kissed his grandfather and cured him of his leprosy:

when he knew that he had been healed by the touch of the infant, [he] rejoiced greatly, like one who had come to a harbour after having suffered shipwreck. And he, who at first was as a roaring lion, was now turned to a lamb, and he began to love the infant above all his sons and grandsons

The Liber landavensis, ed. **Rev. W. J. Rees**, The Welsh MSS. Society, 1840

After many years of teaching, curing the sick and casting out demons – as well as, more prosaically, turning water into wine – Dubricius is thought to have retired to Ynys Enlli (or Bardsey), 'the Isle of Saints', where he died. In 1120, his remains were transferred to Llandaff Cathedral, where his shrine can still be visited today.

HOLY WELLS IN THE AGE OF THE SAINTS

opposite left: St Dubricius' Holy Well, situated in trees just below the Hentland churchyard: St Dubricius' holy well is also known as the 'Lipwell' for its dual troughs, one lip for people and one for animals.
opposite middle: St Dubricius' Church, Hentland
opposite right: The fourteenth century cross, situated in the Hentland churchyard above the well, is thought to portray St Dubricius

above: St Dubricius' Holy Well

BORDERLANDS

Ffynnon Gybi, Llangybi, Monmouthshire

the white hart over the white well *

Ffynnon Gybi
Llangybi, near Newport,
Monmouthshire
OS Landranger Map No.171:
SO 375 966

St Cybi and his company are said to have arrived here from Cornwall in the sixth century, coming ashore from the river Usk. Edelig, the local king, initially tried to eject them but, after being struck blind and his horse felled, the pagan leader quite naturally relented. He was rewarded with the return of his sight (and of his horse) and, in gratitude, gave the saint a hand bell and land upon which to build his churches.

The well itself is said to have erupted at the spot where the saint struck his staff to mark where his first hermitage would be built. This was Llangybi's main water source until 1951 when it fell into steep decline, described by later visitors as merely a pile of toppled stones. Happily, the well was restored by Llangybi Fawr Community Council (with financial help from CADW), and re-dedicated by the Bishop of Monmouth on 21 September 2007.

The Council's efforts in repairing the well and re-establishing the site as a focal point for the community have been justifiably rewarded by an Usk Civic Society Award.

Ffynnon Gybi and the public house above it are now believed to have been the inspiration for TS Eliot's poem 'Usk', which had baffled critics for decades, not recognising that the 'white hart' in question was the name of the hostelry (constructed in the early 1500s, occupied in turn by Henry VIII and Oliver Cromwell, and visited by Eliot in 1935), rather than the animal:

Usk

Do not suddenly break the branch, or
Hope to find
The white hart over the white well.*
Glance aside, not for lance, do not spell
Old enchantments. Let them sleep.
'Gently dip, but not too deep',
Lift your eyes
Where the roads dip and where the roads rise
Seek only there
Where the grey light meets the green air
The Hermit's chapel, the pilgrim's prayer.

TS Eliot

above: White Hart Village Inn, Llangybi

ignoring the portents
holy wells of Ethelbert

Ethelbert I, raised as a worshipper of the pagan god Odin, was the first Anglo-Saxon king to convert to Christianity, probably through a combination of the gentle persuasion of his Frankish wife Bertha, and the powerful intercession of the Roman missionary, Augustine who had arrived along with forty other monks on the Isle of Thanet in Kent in 587 on the instruction of Pope Gregory.

Although initially insisting that the meeting with these men of a new faith took place out of doors so that no sorcery could be performed, the king's conversion was quickly followed by an explosion of Christian church building and campaigns to convert his subjects, which resulted in Ethelbert I's eventual canonisation, following his death in 616.

It is the story of Ethelbert II, however, that we remember in the wells that bear the Ethelbert name in the Borderlands area.

above: The new shrine of beautiful Orthodox-style icons, at the entrance to the Lady Chapel at Hereford Cathedral – designed by Robert Kilgour, the cathedral architect and painted by Peter Murphy in 2007 – tells the story of the life and martyrdom of Hereford's saint at what is believed to be the site of the original shrine to St Ethelbert, destroyed during the Reformation.

caption: left: the river Lugg at St Mary's Church
centre and below: St Ethelbert's Well
inside St Mary's Church, Marden

St Ethelbert's Well

St Mary's Church, Marden,
near Hereford, Herefordshire
OS Explorer Map No.202: SO 512 471

St Mary's Church in Marden, situated on the eastern bank of the river Lugg, a little north of Hereford, houses one of the strangest holy wells in Britain. Surmounted by a bizarre late-Victorian octagonal wooden table structure, the well is located in the floor of an incongruously-carpeted room at the back of the parish church. It also has one of the most extraordinary of tales to tell.

Little is known of the life of Ethelbert II or his late eighth century reign. He was said by some to have been the son of Ethelred I of East Anglia and Leofruna of Mercia, and to have ruled wisely.

In some versions, against his will and in others for love, he had agreed to wed Elfrida, the daughter of King Offa of Mercia, the most powerful Anglo-Saxon king of his day. Setting out to visit his bride-to-be – despite his mother's forebodings and his own discouraging premonitions (which included an earthquake and a solar eclipse!) – the girl's father had Ethelbert killed at the iron-age hillfort known as Sutton Walls, a mile or so south-east of the present-day church.

Some legends claim that an unusual method was used to despatch the potential suitor, a seat-less chair, disguised with a cloth and placed over a deep cellar into which Ethelbert fell.

Here his broken body was strangled and decapitated, his head, it was said, kicked like a football all the way to Marden. Ethelbert's remains were thrown into a hastily-prepared and unmarked grave next to the river Lugg but, soon afterwards, bright lights were observed above the burial place and rumours of Ethelbert's ghost being seen in the area proliferated. King Offa, feeling remorse for his act of barbarity against his would-be son-in-law, asked for absolution from the Pope, who instructed him to pay for the canonisation of Ethelbert, and to build a church to the new saint at the place where his body had been buried.

Such was the press of pilgrims at Marden, however, that the saint's remains were eventually moved to a new and larger shrine at Hereford Cathedral.

When Ethelbert's body was disinterred, a healing well miraculously formed where he had lain, and this is said to be the most-unusual well we see today in St Mary's Church in Marden.

St Ethelbert's Well

Castle Green, Hereford, Herefordshire
OS Explorer Map No.189: SO 509 398

It was claimed that when a blind man tripped over the head of St Ethelbert – when accidentally dropped on its journey to Hereford – he immediately and miraculously regained his sight. And when St Ethelbert's coffin was rested near the end of its passage to its new Cathedral home, another healing spring erupted which for centuries was believed to cure eye infections and ulcers. Sadly, today, this important well, so central to the story of Hereford, is dry, the carved head of the city's saintly patron eroded by human neglect and the weather.

Ethelbert's body was finally buried at Hereford Cathedral which is today dedicated to Our Lady and St Ethelbert and his cult flourished here, becoming at one time second only to Canterbury as a pilgrimage destination.

right: all that is left of the statue of St Ethelbert above his well

the site of St Ethelbert's Well, Hereford

HOLY WELLS IN THE AGE OF THE SAINTS

four of the icon panels at St Ethelbert's new shrine, Hereford Cathedral

the spring in eternity *

holy wells of St Winefride and St Beuno

Winefride (or Gwenfrewi) was a north Wales saint of the seventh century, the daughter of Welsh nobleman Tyfid ap Eiludd and his wife Gwenlo. The architectures of her wells on either side of the Wales / England border offer two of the most contrasting, most beautiful and most interesting of all well sites in Britain. And the incredible stories for which they provide the scenery are of lust, murder, retribution and resurrection.

There are a variety of different versions of the innocent Winefride's tale but all agree that she planned to become a nun, probably alongside her aunt Tenhoi who was the abbess of Gwytherin, near Llanwrst in Denbighshire. One day, so it is said, a local chieftain's son, one Caradoc stopping on his journey, tired and thirsty, asked Winefride for a drink, and, looking into her eyes, fell immediately in love. Some say he asked her to marry him on the spot; others that he was already married and that his intentions were much less honourable. Whatever the case, she refused him and he tried to take her by force. Enraged by her rejection, Caradoc took out his sword and cut off her head.

As a result, it is said, of her purity and goodness, a great spring immediately erupted out of the ground at the very spot where her head fell. This was to become the elaborate shrine of St Winefride at Holywell:

... the ground stained with her blood cracked, and a rapid spring gushed out in that place full of water, the stones of which to this day are seen bloody as on the first day.

translation from the Latin, from anon., *First Life*, c.1130

Luckily for Winefride, however, her maternal uncle Beuno was celebrating mass in his small wooden chapel nearby and was able to replace the head and restore her to life. Caradog, in contrast, cursed by Beuno (something at which he seems to have been very skilled, as we will see later) was taken by the devil, melting slowly and painfully into the earth, never to be seen again.

After the ordeal, the chroniclers reported that Winefride returned to her religious vocation, first founding a convent near Holywell, before joining her aunt at Gwytherin, and eventually becoming the abbess there herself, where she eventually died and was buried in 660.

top: This statue of St Winefride at Holywell dates from the 1880s, replacing the original which was destroyed during the Reformation.
middle: Another 1888 statue of the saint is set above the inner pool altar.

above: stained glass window at St Winefride's showing Winefride, Beuno and the well: note Beuno's crude cosmetic surgery on the neck of Winefride.

HOLY WELLS IN THE AGE OF THE SAINTS

the bathing pool and pilgrims' changing tents at St Winefride's

BORDERLANDS

below: discarded crutches in the museum at St Winefride's

opposite: St Winefride Well'

After her death and following countless reports of miraculous cures at her well, a major Winefride cult developed and, by 1138, such was her popularity that her remains were transferred to Shrewsbury Abbey and thousands visited both Shrewsbury and Holywell annually to pay their respects and to seek guidance and healing. Legend tells of one miraculous cure during the relics' journey to Shrewsbury when a man took a pinch of dust from St Winefride's skull, mixed it with water and gave it to a sick man to drink … with astonishing results:

… many times this most benign virgin relieves dropsical persons, restores the paralytic, heals the gouty, cures the melancholy. No less does she remove sciatica, eradicate cancer, cure shortness of breath, extirpate piles…

The Life of St Wenefred
in **A.W. Wade-Evans'** *Vitae Sanctorum Britanniae et Genealogiae*, 1944

During the Reformation, Wales, in particular, was seen as being "in an evil condition as to religion, the inhabitants remaining still greatly ignorant and superstitious" (Archbishop Parker of Canterbury, 1564), and so was set in trail the attack on "all nefarious conventicles of the wicked and the superstitious dogmas of the papists" (Bishop, 1576).

Nearly all of Winefride's many relics were destroyed during this time, including in 1540, her magnificent shrine at Shrewsbury Abbey. The sole surviving remnant is part of her skeleton, too small to be properly identified but believed to be part of the saint's finger bone, which is now housed, appropriately, at Holywell where her story began.

St Winefride's Well
Holywell, Flintshire
OS Landranger Map No.116:
SJ 185 763

in water in deep devotion up to their chins for hours, sending up their prayers

Thomas Pennant, 1781

With more than 1,300 years of continuous recorded Christian usage, St Winefride's Well in Holywell – known as 'The Lourdes of Wales' – is the grandest well building in the British Isles.

Its elaborate and impressive two-storeyed late fifteenth and early sixteenth century Late Perpendicular Gothic construction with star-shaped well, large bathing pool and first-floor chapel have all survived almost intact since their completion in 1512 under the leadership of Abbot Pennant of Basingwek. St Winefride's shrine escaped the terminal attacks inflicted upon many other Catholic holy centres during the Reformation (including that at Shrewsbury), such was its perceived importance, its money-generating potential, and the regularity of its delivery of seemingly verifiable cures:

Hundred of sick folk who have arrived on crutches, but who can run back home.

anon, *The Miracles of Wales*, 1820

In 1189, Richard I visited this calcium and iron rich spring, as, on later occasions, did his successors, Henry V (who, in 1416, arrived on foot to give thanks for his victory at Agincourt), Edward IV and James II, the latter in the company of his queen to ask for a son, a wish that was granted soon afterwards in 1688. And the young Princess, later to become Queen Victoria visited the well while on holiday in the area in the 1820s.

Probably the most famous 'cure' recorded at Holywell was that of Winefrid White. Here is the 1806 testimony of the surgeon Samuel Stubbs, reported in **J Milner**'s *Authentic Documents relative to the Miraculous Cure of Winefrid White, of Wolverhampton, at St. Winefrid's Well…On the 28th of June 1805*:

I first visited the aforesaid Winefrid White … Sept. 1, 1802; at which time, … I found her in a very debilitated and languishing state, owing to an internal disorder, accompanied with the most fatal symptoms. These brought on an enlargement of the vertebrae, with a relaxation of the ligaments, and a paralytic affection, particularly of the left side; so that, at length, the patient could not hold herself upright, nor move herself from place to place, except in the most feeble manner, and by the help of a crutch…I have frequently seen her and conversed with her since, without discovering any change in her for the better, down to the 22d or 23d of last June; being two or three days before she is reported to have made a journey to Holywell … All the above mentioned fatal symptoms … have disappeared. The ligaments of the vertebrae are contracted and firm, as I ascertained yesterday…These changes so extraordinary, compleat, and performed in so short a time, I am unable to account for, by any principle of medicine I am acquainted with, or by any experience I have had in it.

And, more than a decade later, to prove the case:

The aforesaid Wenefride White is living at the present day, in a state of perfect health, and now superintends a Catholic charity school in Wolverhampton…The witnesses to the above cure are numerous and consist of persons of different stations, religions, countries, and places of residence, with Protestants, Catholics, English, Welsh, residents in Wolverhampton, Liverpool, and Holywell, who could not possibly be combined for the purpose of attesting a series of falsehoods.

Fr Metcalf, from *The Life and Miracles of Saint Wenefride*, 1817

Others visited for spiritual uplift alone or to seek confirmation of their faiths. This is the journal entry for 8 October 1874 of the poet-priest Gerard Manley Hopkins:

Barraud and I walked over to Holywell and bathed at the well and returned very joyously. The sight of the water in the well as clear as glass, greenish like beryl or aquamarine at the surface with the force of the springs, and shaping out the five foils of the well quite drew and held my eyes to it.

The strong unfailing flow of the water and the chain of cures from year to year all these centuries took hold of my mind with wonder at the bounty of God in one of His saints, the sensible thing so naturally and gracefully uttering the spiritual reason of its being … and the spring in place leading back the thoughts by its spring in time to its spring in eternity … *

This is a site of international importance that is still visited by more than 36,000 people annually, a figure, we are told, that is increasing year on year. Today, a diverse range of pilgrims make their way to Holywell, including those growing in number who have, according to David Birchall of the St Beuno's Ignatian Spirituality Centre in Tremierchion "a spiritual need but do not want to join churches", a large proportion in my experience of the well-hunting fraternity:

In cities that
have outgrown their promise people
are becoming pilgrims
again, if not to this place,
then to the recreation of it
in their own spirits.

RS Thomas
from 'The Moon in Lleyn'
from the collection *Laboratories of the Spirit*, 1975

opposite near:
St Winefride's Well, Holywell opposite far:
imagines of pilgrims emersing themselves
– voluntarily and otherwise – in the waters
at St Winefride's Well

St Winefride's Well
Woolston, near Oswestry, Shropshire
Landranger Map No.126: SJ 322 244

It is said that, on its way to re-interment at Shrewsbury Abbey in 1138, Winefride's body rested overnight in the hamlet of Woolston near Oswestry, where a spring miraculously erupted out of the ground. The waters at Woolston are claimed to be especially good at healing bruises, wounds and broken bones.

The well is covered by a fine fifteenth century half-timbered cottage beneath which the waters flow through a series of stone troughs – some with niches to hold offerings and statues of the saint – then on, into a large ornamental pond.

In later years, the site was converted into a private plunge bath, then a public bath until it was forced to close in 1755 'riotous conduct' which was claimed to be taking place there.

The cottage is currently owned, managed and rented out by the Landmark Trust.

left: 'a cross of blood', beneath the waters at St Winefride's Well, Woolston, near Oswestry

opposite near: St Winefride's Well and cottage
opposite far: views of the cottage interior and from the cottage kitchen, St Winefride's Well

HOLY WELLS IN THE AGE OF THE SAINTS

BORDERLANDS

above: offerings left att Winefride's
middle: the inner well, below the house
below: St Winefride's Well
right: St Winefride's Well pool and gardens

HOLY WELLS IN THE AGE OF THE SAINTS

cure and curse

Beuno (c.545-640), Winefride's uncle, seems to have been one of Wales' most widely-travelled saints, journeying the length and breadth of the country practising his strange combination of magical skills. On the one hand, his untrustworthy legend paints him as bringing as many as seven people back to life (including his niece); while on the other, he was renowned as a great curser.

On one occasion, his famous temper was unleashed upon the grandsons of Cynan, the king of Powys, who had arrived at his home in Gwyddelwern expecting the normal Welsh rites of hospitality. Beuno – unhappy at having to kill one of his young oxen for the benefit of these unwanted guests, and at their subsequent reception of his cooking which they claimed had been purposely blighted by their host – violently cursed the young men in a manner that would make the chef Gordon Ramsay proud:

May your kin never possess the land, and may you be destroyed out of this kingdom and be likewise deprived of your eternal inheritance!

As the antiquarian Rev Sabine Baring-Gould later observed: "... it was a risky thing to interfere with these old Celtic saints, who wielded the keys of Heaven in a very arbitrary fashion." (*The Lives of the Saints,* 1872)

Having studied for the priesthood from a very early age, Beuno - following his father's death - founded his first church in Llanymynech, a village which straddles the border between Montgomeryshire / Powys and Shropshire, which runs down the middle of the main road for most of its length. The now closed Lion pub here had within it two bars in England and one in Wales, allowing for the short trip across the establishment to 'wet' Shropshire from 'dry' Montgomeryshire on a Sunday when laws prohibited selling alcohol on the Sabbath in Wales.

Beuno is said to have added to Llanmynech's highly polarised atmosphere when he planted a magical oak tree over his father's grave which could distinguish between the Welsh and the English, allowing the former to pass under it safely but trapping the latter within its branches!

The saint established his next church at Berriew on land granted to him by the king, despite Beuno's ungracious treatment of his family members. Being too close in his mind to the English here, however, he moved north to Meifod, then on further north again to Gwyddelwern where Cynan again provided the land for yet another church building. It was here that his first act of bringing the dead back to life was reported, the lucky recipient being an Irishman named Llorcan Wyddel.

Despite Beuno's contradictory natures, he is considered by some to be the patron saint of north Wales ... as well as that of sick children and diseased cattle.

right: Ffynnon Beuno, Tremeirchion, Denbighshire

BORDERLANDS

Ffynnon Beuno
Tremeirchion, near St Asaph,
Denbighshire
Landranger Map No.116: SJ 083 723

The water which emerges here from the gaping mouth of a stone head may be a sculptural reference to Beuno's ability to reverse the violence of decapitation, as well as an allusion to the ancient Celtic cult of the head upon which his practises were historically based. This is certainly a site which links us to our earliest ancestors: in caves in the small valley beyond the old well house, the bones of sixteen different animals, including mammoth, woolly rhinoceros, hyena, elk, wolf and cave lion, and a flint tool carbon dated to 38,000 BC have been unearthed.

The water from Ffynnon Beuno was believed to be efficacious in the healing of rheumatism, sore eyes, warts, eczema, epilepsy and paralysis if drunk or immersed within. The large one-metre-deep bathing pool and the substantial house – which became a pub and a shop, after its first outing as the well guardian's cottage – all attest, along with the ancient caves, to its long history of usage for a wide variety of pilgrims and those in need of a cure.

above: the gaping mouth of St Winefride at Ffynnon Beuno, Tremeirchion ?

opposite: Ffynnon Beuno well guardian's cottage, kneeler from the Church of Corpus Christi depicting the well and cottage, the interior of the well and the well pump, Tremeirchion

opposite far: Ffynnon Beuno, Gwyddelwern, near Corwen, Denbighshire

HOLY WELLS IN THE AGE OF THE SAINTS

Ffynnon Beuno
Gwyddelwern, near Corwen,
Denbighshire
OS Explorer Map No.264: SJ 077 465

During St Beuno's travels throughout north Wales, he is thought to have left behind five wells, another of which is at Gwyddelwern. Both church and well here are in very poor states of repair, the former unsafe and closed to visitors, and the well neglected and overgrown, crudely fenced beside the main A494 Corwen to Ruthin road.

From his church here at Gwyddelwern, Beuno moved on again, back to Flintshire where he was to play his major role in the history of holy wells by restoring Winefride's head at Holywell.

The saint finally settled at Clynnog Fawr on the Llyn Peninsula in Gwynedd, founding churches and restoring lives there and across the Menai Straits on Anglesey until his death in 640.

BORDERLANDS

beautiful and luminous bones *

St Milburga's Wells

St Milburga was one of three daughters of Merewald, a high-ranking Herefordshire nobleman, part of the royal house of Mercia, and the youngest son of the pagan king Penda. Born in 664 and educated in Paris, Milburga was to become a powerful Saxon princess and a devout abbess of Much Wenlock Priory … as well as a miracle worker.

Her reputation was based upon such incredible acts as bringing a dead boy back to life, curing lepers and even "hanging her veil on a sunbeam", no easy feat! She communed with animals, once successfully ordering a flock of birds to stop stealing her monastery's crops. And, of course, she made water miraculously erupt from the earth.

Wenlock Priory
Much Wenlock, Shropshire
OS Explorer Map No.217: SO 625 001

I do love these ancient ruins
We never set foot upon them but we set
Our foot upon some reverend history.
And questionless, here in this open court,
Which now lies naked to the injuries
Of stormy weather, some men lie interr'd
Lov'd the church so well, and gave largely to 't
They thought it should have canopy'd their bones
Till doomsday

John Webster (c.1580-c.1634), from the play *The Duchess of Malfi* (1612/13)

Milburga's father, Merewald built the first religious house here in 680 and his daughter became its second abbess in 687, in charge of both its monks and its nuns (a not un-common practise at the time).

This construction was completely destroyed by the Danes sometime in the ninth century, cementing the description of King Ethelred as 'the Unready' as he and his large army were peacefully encamped nearby!

The site was resurrected in the mid eleventh century, this time as a college of priests, built by Earl Loefric and his wife Lady Godgifu (better known as Godiva). It then became a priory when French monks were sent to Wenlock at the request of Roger of Montgomery after the Norman Conquest.

HOLY WELLS IN THE AGE OF THE SAINTS

below: Wenlock Priory, Much Wenlock

opposite far: part of the tiled floor in the Library, Wenlock Priory
opposite middle: the remains of the decorative lavabo (built in 1220) where the monks washed their hands before eating, Priory Cloister, Much Wenlock
opposite near: arches leading to the Chapter House, Wenlock Priory

In the year 1101, the remains of the famous abbess were said to have been discovered here by two boys who disappeared into a pit of "beautiful and luminous bones" * while playing in the ruins.

Milburga's miracles multiplied from that day on and Wenlock became an important place of pilgrimage during the twelfth century. Chroniclers claimed that even the water in which her skeleton was washed could effect miracles, after a woman suffering from a mysterious wasting disease drank some of the liquid and vomited a great worm and was cured!

What we see today at Wenlock Priory is mostly the remains of works of the thirteenth century and later, destroyed during Henry VIII's Dissolution of the Monasteries when, in 1540, the site was stripped of all of its valuables and its buildings sold. Sadly, there is no trace today of the once impressive shrine of St Milburga.

St Milburga's most revealing adventures concern her many conflicts with the Celtic tribes who were her often-troublesome neighbours. Legend tells that, out riding one evening on her white mule, the nun was spotted by pagan tribesmen from the other side of the border … with mischief on their minds. Milburga represented the new faith, the Welsh the old, and this tale is symbolic of the tension between the two, written in this case from an Anglo-Saxon perspective.

The Welsh with their swift horses and powerful pack of hounds pursued Milburga - fleeing for her life and for her religion - until she reached the church of St Peter on the Corve river at Stanton Lacy where she prayed to the saint who caused a flood to wash away the Welsh.

After spending the night in the safety of the church, she set out the next morning to find her way home, but the pagans were waiting for her, angered at their failure to punish the high-ranking Christian intruder the previous day … and gave chase again. And again Milburga's mule outpaced their steeds, until after hours of riding (some say days!), she fell from her horse, fatigued, and cracked her head on a rock, crimson now with her blood, a stain many claimed to have seen in the centuries that followed.

Observing her fall, a group of men (some versions say only two) sowing barley in a nearby field rushed to Milburga's aid. And it was said that, as there was no water to cleanse the young woman's wound, she asked her mount to strike the ground three times with its hoof, and, as it did, water flowed freely … and still does to this day.

In thanks for their help, Milburga commanded the barley that the men had only just sown to grow to its full height, and asked the workers to provide one more service to her: "When the Welsh and their hounds arrive, as they very soon will, they will ask you if you have seen me. I do not want you to lie, so tell them, 'Yes, we have seen her. She was here last when we sowed this field'."

When her pursuers drew near, the men did as they were asked and the Welsh gave up the chase, confused and questioning their sanity. It is said that later, when they heard the tale of a field sown and harvested in the same day by the agency of a Christian god, they abandoned their ancient faith and were baptised.

left: the ruins of Wenlock Priory

opposite: St Peter's Church, Stanton Lacy, near Ludlow, where St Milburga rested after her pursuit by the pagan Welsh

HOLY WELLS IN THE AGE OF THE SAINTS

HOLY WELLS IN THE AGE OF THE SAINTS

St Milburga's Well
Stoke St Milborough, Shropshire
OS Explorer Map No.217: SO 568 823

This beautifully-situated site is said to be the place where Milburga fell from her horse and created a new well with which to wash her wounds.

At the foot of the steep bank leading up Brown Clee Hill, a little above the church, this is an unfailing spring, reputed to be good for sore eyes. Its waters, it is claimed were also in much demand for 'bucking', a medieval practise for washing linen and clothes using – prior to the general availability of soap – hot water with bleaching agents such as wood ashes, bran or sometimes even stale urine and dung!

opposite: steps leading down to
St Milburga's Well, Stoke St Milborogh

right top: the entrance to
St Milburga's Well
other images: St Milburga's Well

121

St Milburga's Well

Much Wenlock, Shropshire
OS Explorer Map No.217: SO 625 988

There are two wells dedicated to St Milburga in Much Wenlock. This one, off Barrow Street near the entrance to the Priory ruins is said to have supplied a carved fountain within the Abbey precincts which has recently been unearthed.

Now dry, the water from the well would once have filled the basin to the current ground level to allow full body emersion. In addition to its healing properties, it could provide, it is claimed, husbands for young girls if visited on the right day of the year and its waters dabbed on the face!

St Milburga died sometime between 722 and 730, in her sixties, most unusual for the time.

cynhafal the obscure

Ffynnon Gynhafal

Llangynhafal, near Ruthin, Denbighshire
OS Explorer Map No.265: SJ 133 638

Cynhafal was probably a seventh century Welsh monk and the church here on the lower slopes of the Clwydian Hills is the only one in the whole of Wales dedicated to this most obscure of saints. Its circular churchyard suggests a pre-Christian origin.

The substantial holy well itself, in the garden of the adjacent farm against the breath-taking backdrop of Moel Famau, was renowned for banishing warts and relieving rheumatism.

You were required to prick your warts with a pin which you then threw into the waters, accompanied by a prayer to the saint.

left: St Milburga's Well, Much Wenlock

opposite: Ffynnon Gynhafal

HOLY WELLS IN THE AGE OF THE SAINTS

HOLY WELLS IN THE AGE OF THE SAINTS

hanging his coat on a sunbeam

St Chad's Wells

Chad was born in Northumbria. He was trained by St Aidan on the Isle of Lindisfarne, graduating at the age of thirty as a priest in the Celtic Church in Ireland, and was appointed Bishop of Mercia in 669. Settling in Lichfield, he built his oratory here and baptised converts in the local spring, where Bede claimed he also prayed naked, standing on a stone in the cold waters.

It was said that Chad helped convert King Penda of Mercia after he had killed his rival King Oswald at Winwick (see St Oswald's Well, p.148). But the story of his conversion of another Mercian sovereign is particularly colourful:

Chad loved animals. Such was his empathy with the plight of all of God's creatures that he would insist upon walking everywhere, irrespective of the distance, not to burden a horse or a mule.

opposite: the Llangynhafal Church window, 'stained' only by nature

right: wooden statue of St Chad, Romiley, near Stockport, Cheshire

125

BORDERLANDS

One day, alone in his cell by his well, a deer came to drink from the gentle saint's waters, took his fill and departed. Wulfhade, the son of King Wulfhere of Mercia, in pursuit of the deer asked St Chad if he had seen his prey, to which Chad replied that the animal had been sent that way by God to lead Wulfhade to him to hear the Christian gospel. Wulfhade laughed at the saint's presumption and replied that he would be more likely to abandon paganism if Chad's prayers to his god could bring back the deer. Chad duly obliged and the creature walked slowly out of the forest and stood next to the saint. On witnessing this, Wulfhade fell at Chad's feet and asked for the saint's forgiveness, and for immediate baptism. Later, Wulfhade brought his brother Rufine to Chad and he too, it was said, converted to Christianity.

Wulfhere, their father the pagan king, on hearing this news, slew both of his sons in anger, but later, in remorse, also sought out St Chad and his well. On reaching his cell, it was reported that the saint greeted Wulfhere warmly, and taking off his vestments hung them on a sunbeam – like St Milburga – filling the room with heavenly light. Seeing this, the king himself converted and St Chad instructed him to destroy all of his heathen shrines and to build monasteries in their stead.

below: St Chad's Church, Lichfield
opposite: St Chad's Well, Romiley

126

St Chad's Well

Chadkirk, Romiley, near Stockport,
Greater Manchester
OS Explorer Map No.109: SJ 937 908

Half a mile south of the centre of Romiley, Chadkirk offers a seventeenth century farm house, a Victorian walled garden and a sixteenth century chapel amidst ancient woodlands.

And there is also a revived 'tradition' of well-dressing here, at St Chad's Well, now supported by Stockport Metropolitan Borough Council.

St Chad's Well

St Chad's Church, Lichfield, Staffordshire
OS Landranger Map No.128: SK 122 103

St Chad's Well in Lichfield, in the grounds of St Chad's Church, is a rather unimpressive 1949 replacement for an arched stone well house which itself replaced a much earlier building based, it is said, upon the wooded site where Chad once baptised his converts.

The vines which currently cover the canopy symbolise the Eucharistic wine, and the well is dressed with flowers and greenery on Holy Thursday, at a site reveered by both Anglicans and Catholics.

Chad – flanked by the saints Peada and Wulfhere – in the nineteenth century scultures above the western entrance of Lichfield Cathedral

St Chad's Well, Lichfield

statue of St Chad in the porch of St Chad's Church, Lichfield, Staffordshire

HOLY WELLS IN THE AGE OF THE SAINTS

the magnificent western entrance to Lichfield Cathedral, Staffordshire

opposite left: the nave, Lichfield Cathedral
opposite above: the so-called 'Head Chapel' in Lichfield Cathedral where the bones of the saint were kept and exhibited to pilgrims up to the year 1540
opposite below: St Chad's (underwhelming) 'Shrine' at Lichfield Cathedral

right: St Chad window, Chester Cathedral

St Chad died on 2 March 672 and, in the year 700, his bones were transferred to Lichfield Cathedral, a place of pilgrimage, along with his well, and of many reported miraculous cures from then onwards.

(Chad's remains were later moved again to the Roman Catholic Cathedral in Birmingham.)

BORDERLANDS

he saw his murder in a dream *

the holy wells of St Kenelm

In our sweet shires of Mercia
Five blessed Saints we had;
Four were proud Princes of the Church,
And one was a little lad.

Wistan, Wulstan, Oswald, Chad:
Each hallowed Mercia's realm;
But the saint we love all others above
Is little Saint Kenelm.

Francis Brett Young, from 'The Ballad of St Kenelm AD 821', from *The Island*, 1944

The story of Kenelm – prince, short-lived king and martyr – comes to us originally from a manuscript found at Winchcombe Abbey which itself is said to have been based upon a twelfth century account given by a Worcester monk named Wilfin. As is often the case, a number of alternative versions are available.

The most popular tells of how King Kenwulph of Mercia died leaving two daughters, Quendryda and Burgenhilda, and a son named Kenelm, a child of just seven years old who inherited the throne. Given the boy's age, his sister Quendryda and her lover Ascobert were entrusted with his guardianship.

We twain are one in will and flesh,
And but for one small thing
I should have been thy crowned queen
And thou my wedded king;

And that small thing is but the breath
Of my father's brat, Kenelm.
Give me his life, and wed me wife,
And we will share this realm!

the north window (made in memory of the child victims of the First World War) telling the story of St Kenelm's short life, St Kenelm's Church, Romsley

Quendryda and Ascobert first tried to poison the young monarch and when that failed, they arranged for a hunting 'accident' in the forests of the Clent Hills.

The night before the fateful trip, Kenelm had a worrying dream. He was climbing a giant tree "that reached to the stars", richly decorated with flowers and lanterns, from the top of which he could see all four corners of his kingdom. Three bowed down to him, but the fourth took up axes and chopped at the base, and as the tree fell, Kenelm became a white bird and flew into the sky.

Relating his dream to Ascobert the next morning, he was reassured by the treacherous lord that it was an omen of good luck for the hunt, although his nanny, a wise old woman gifted in the interpretation of dreams, knew of its real meaning.

On the first day of the hunt while Kenelm rested, Ascobert dug the young king's grave beside his sleeping body, but the boy awoke and – recognising Ascobert's evil intension – told his assassin that he would not be slain there but in another place. He thrust his stick into the ground and it instantly began to blossom, growing in years to come into a great ash tree known as St Kenelm's Ash. As the child sang the *Te Deum*, Ascobert took the king deeper into the forests of the Clent Hills, and there cut off his head, burying him where he fell.

… when they came to a woodland brook,
And the child, unaware,
Knelt by the brink and bent to drink,
A sword flashed in the air;

* Geoffrey Chaucer, from *The Nun's Priest's Tale*, *The Canterbury Tales*, late fourteenth century

HOLY WELLS IN THE AGE OF THE SAINTS

And the shorn head of little Kenelm
Reddened the brook with blood,
While Escebert leapt to his saddle and crept
Like a wolf from Offa's Wood.

But, just as the dream had foretold, Kenelm's soul rose up in the form of a dove. Carrying a scroll, it flew all the way to Rome, eventually dropping it at the feet of the Pope. The message read: 'Low in a mead of kine under a thorn, of head bereft, lieth poor Kenelm king-born'.

The Pope immediately wrote to the Archbishop of Canterbury, who sent out men from the Mercian capital, Winchcombe, to find the body.

And when they came to the woods of Clent
And rode into the shade,
Behold a shaft of blinding light
Fell where the child was laid!

One version of the story says that they were guided to the boy and the blood-stained sword by a pillar of light shining from the grave up to the heavens; another that the spot was marked by a cow, which did not eat or drink but never went hungry, standing guard over a thorn bush.

Either way, a fountain of healing waters burst forth out of the ground at the place where the young king's body was disinterred.

scenes from St Kenelm's life, St Kenelm's Church window, Romsley: Kenelm's dream; his murder at the hands of Ascobert; the saint's discovery; the cow and the thorn bush; Quendryda's death

BORDERLANDS

St Kenelm's Well
near Romsley, Clent Hills,
Worcestershire
OS Explorer Map No.219: SO 945 807

There is much debate about the exact location of the holy well where Kenelm was beheaded by Ascobert.

Now sensitively-landscaped with paths, and dressed with sculptures and carvings (by the artist Michael Fairfax, working with local adults and children), the Clent Hills' site has lost none of its power to move and to inspire, sitting as it does in a dell below the young martyred saint's church.

above: St Kenelm's Church, near Romsley
right: St Kenelm's Well

HOLY WELLS IN THE AGE OF THE SAINTS

below: the 1985 brick well housing at St Kenelm's

left: ribbons and other 'clouties' near St Kenelm's Well, Clent Hills

135

BORDERLANDS

There was even more drama on the sixty-mile journey of Kenelm's body to its final resting place, some claiming that at every stop a new healing spring emerged … and the deaf, the blind and the lame were healed.

While the new young saint's body was carried towards Winchcombe, its bearers were approached by a set of rival claimants to the remains – an armed band from Worcester Abbey – at the ford called Pyriford over the River Avon.

It was finally agreed that whichever party woke first the following morning would win the right to take and display the remains, a hugely rewarding privilege in those days. Although the monks from Winchcombe prevailed, setting off before sunrise, they were pursued by the Worcester Abbey men. Stopping within sight of Winchcombe, exhausted and thirsty from their march, they struck their staffs into the ground and another miraculous spring burst forth to enable them to complete their journey.

left: It is thought that this crossing of the Avon near Pershore was the spot where the quarrel between the Winchcombe and the Worcester men took place.

above: the nave, Pershore Abbey, Pershore, Worcestershire

St Kenelm's Well

near Winchcombe, Sudeley Hill,
near Cheltenham, Gloucestershire
OS Explorer Map No.OL45:
SP 044 278

...it is very pleasant to imagine the picturesque groups of devout worshippers and gay holiday lads and lasses which must have then assembled on St Kenelm's day (July 17th) even round our Sudeley Well and Chapel. It may be right in this matter of fact, prosaic, and scientific age to condemn such superstitions as we are now recording, but when there was more of nature and less of dogma in religion, it seems hardly surprising that a beautiful fountain of clear water, ever flowing, ever fresh – no one then knowing whence it came, or whither it flowed – should inspire the worship of the people.

Emma Dent from *Annals of Winchcombe and Sudeley*, 1877

St Kenelm's Holy Well,
Sudeley Hill, Winchcombe

BORDERLANDS

The impressive Grade II Listed well house structure on Sudeley Hill was built during the reign of Elizabeth I and restored in Victorian times by JD Wyatt, when the effigy of the saint was placed above the door in the Jubilee year of 1887.

It was here that Kenelm's young body was thought to have rested for the very last time before its final triumphant return to Winchcombe.

right: the 1887 'St Kenelmus' statue above the entrance to St Kenelm's Holy Well, near Winchcombe

HOLY WELLS IN THE AGE OF THE SAINTS

St Kenelm's Holy Well

left and below:
inside St Kenelm's Well

below: lower St Kenelm's Well

HOLY WELLS IN THE AGE OF THE SAINTS

On finally arriving at Winchcombe, it was claimed that the bells rang out, "without the hand of man". And, as the saint's body entered the town – to be buried alongside his father in the Abbey – Kenelm's sister Quendryda and her lover Escobert received their just deserts:

… as through Winchcombe's mourning street
They passed by slow degrees,
Quendrytha at her window sate
With the Bible on her knees.

She read of false Queen Jezebel,
And when they spied the hearse
That carried Kenelm, her wicked eyes
Spat blood upon the verse.
…..
And Escebert, her foul paramour,
They slew him where he stood;
And those twain lay for a week and a day,
And the dogs lapped their blood.

left: entrance to Winchcombe Abbey
above: What little now remains of Winchcombe Abbey
- destroyed during Reformation - is on private land.
A nineteenth century cross now marks the place
where the Abbey once stood.

While digging in the Abbey grounds in 1815, two stone coffins were unearthed, believed to be those of King Kenwulf and his son St Kenelm.

The fact that one was large and the other small added credence to the belief.

above: what is thought by some to be St Kenwulf's stone coffin

below: the much smaller St Kenelm's coffin, both now displayed in the parish church of St Peter in Winchcombe

As we have seen before, medieval hagiographers never let historical fact get in the way of a good story! Various authorities suggest that Kenelm became king at the age of twelve, and that he was twenty-five at the time of his death, not seven. Records also indicate that Kenelm's sister had entered a cloister at the time of her father's passing, and was the abbess of Minster-in-Thanet, an unlikely calling for a murderess!

But the popular saint and his dramatic and uplifting story was good for business, both ecclesiastical as well as financial:

the waters that well from where he fell
All mortal ills assuage
Not even Saint Thomas of Canterbury
Hath greater pilgrimage

Within one hundred years of his 'murder', veneration for Kenelm had spread throughout Britain and into Europe. New miracles were attributed to him – often returning people's sight or sense of hearing, or straightening the bent and the crippled, as well as inflicting severe punishments upon those who did not respect the saint's day – and by the tenth century, Kenelm's legend had made Winchcombe a major centre for pilgrimage.

less of nature / more of dogma

After 1066, Anglo-Norman dominance eventually ended the Celtic ecclesiastical mission of the Age of the Saints, as Welsh bishops were replaced by Norman ones, Celtic monasteries were taken over by Benedictine 'Black' or Cistercian 'White Monks', and the dedications of Celtic saints substituted for those recognised by Rome.

But, although the eventual downfall of the British Church at the hands of the Roman was inevitable, the emphasis upon a more communal ideal, and on the valuing of the natural world and of its sacred waters which the pagan Celts had infused into the new faith – what Emma Dent has described as "more of nature and less of dogma" – endured:

For many centuries Cross and Magic cohabited ... and the faith of the people was a rich palimpsest, one belief layered upon another, reaching back to the earliest atavistic convictions of the Neoliths.

Jan Morris, from *Wales: Epic Views of a Small Country*, 1984

The merging of Celtic thinking with the Christian faith would never be that difficult when, according to the bard Taliesin, writing as far back as the sixth century:

Christ the Word from the beginning was from the beginning our teacher and... there never was a time when the Druids of Britain held not its doctrines.

Seeing holiness and the spiritual everywhere, the Celtic Church provided an essential counterbalance to the more materialistic philosophy of much of the rest of Christendom, championing the rights of community and cultural independence:

Celtic philosophers strove not for the mastery of the world, the imposition of will or the concept of imperial continuity; the goal that was sought was an inner illumination, the growth of spiritual awareness within the external world.

Through their ancient religion, and then with the new vibrancy of Celto-Christianity, they applauded the battle of the individual against outside domination. The individual struggle was a portion of the battle against the oppression of empires; the state; between light and darkness; good and evil; spirituality and materialism; above all ... a constant exuberant celebration of the expression of Free Will.

Peter Berresford Ellis, from *Celtic Inheritance*, 1985

left: fellow pilgrim Susie Warner resting below St Kenelm's well house

* UNDER THE BARBED STING OF ENGLISH LAW
holy wells in the age of the warrior princes

Borders shift, acre by stolen acre.
History dissolves from a nation's
memory, till the story
and the language of that place
turn to a mouthful of stones.

Gillian Clarke, from the poem
'The Map' in *Owain Glyndŵr 1400 – 2000*

After the Romans left Britain in 410 AD, new waves of invaders from Europe – Angles, Saxons, Jutes and Franks, and others from the Nordic seas – forced those on both sides of the border together, united, at least for a short period, against a common foe.

This was an era of alliances but also of betrayals, of small kingdoms and tribal states, and of leaders whose legends would resonate for centuries in the minds of a land desperately seeking the confidence of an independent identity.

This was the time of the mythical Arthur, the scourge of the Saxons; of the warrior king, Rhodri Mawr ('Rhodri the Great') who repelled Viking advances and planted early notions of the possibilities of a Welsh state; of the Welsh law maker, Hywel Dda ('Hywel the Good') who united, albeit temporarily, most of Wales during his reign; and of the warrior saints Tewdrig and Oswald who, like many others, had holy wells associated with their names.

Having themselves initially resisted the advances of Christianity, the converted tribes of the British Borderlands were now employed to stand firm against new pagan invaders from the north and east, and to pass on their newly-acquired faith through word and, where that failed, through bloody deed.

The line from Cardiff to Shrewsbury runs along the Marches, with the plains of England on the one side and the hill country of Wales on the other. I was often stirred on seeing these hills rising in the west. Sometimes night would fall before we reached Ludlow. Westward the sky would be ablaze, reminding one of the battles of the past. Against that radiance the hills rose dark and threatening as if full of armed men waiting for a chance to attack.

RS Thomas from 'The Paths Gone By'

opposite: a view from Raglan Castle, Monmouthshire

above: the great fifteenth century gatehouse at Raglan Castle

* RS Thomas from The Tree / Owain Glyn-Dwr Speaks

in defence of christianity

St Tewdrig's Well
Mathern, near Chepstow, Monmouthshire
OS Explorer Map OL14: ST 523 912

RS Thomas once observed that in the Borderlands "the scent of dead heroes and dead saints" often intermingled.

Tewdrig ap Teithfallt, sovereign of the post-Roman kingdom of Glywysin, was wounded in a battle against the pagan Saxons at Pont y Saeson near Tintern in the year 600, "in Defence of the Christian Religion". Tewdrig had previously handed his crown over to his son Meurig in order to live as a hermit but was forced out of military retirement – despite his advancing age – by the threat to his kingdom … and to his faith.

Tewgrig was victorious, but suffered a head wound in the battle. Chroniclers reported that as he fell two yoked stags emerged from the forest to draw his body to its final resting place. He had wanted to be buried on Ynys Echni (Flat Holm), a favourite graveyard for saints , but got no further than Mathern near Chepstow, where he died.

It was said that, wherever the stags halted, fountains of pure water gushed forth to wash his wounds, the greatest of all being that at Mathern, itself, where his holy well can still be visited.

The place became known as Merthyr Tewdrig (the burial-place of Tewdrig the martyr), and later Mateyrn (place of a king) or Mathern.

Tewdrig's defence of his homeland ensured that the Saxons would not invade this part of Wales again for more than three decades.

In 1881, during renovations to the church at Mathern, an ancient stone coffin was discovered which was reported to contain bones and a fractured skull, believed by many to be those of the Celtic Christian martyr king.

left above: St Tewdrig's Well, Mathern
left below: St Tewdrig's Church, built on the spot where the warrior was said to have died

opposite: wooden statue of St Tewdrig at Mathern

BORDERLANDS

an offering to woden
St Oswald's Wells

Oswald was the early seventh century king of Northumbria who had converted to Christianity at Iona in Scotland and was defeated in battle by Penda, the pagan King of Mercia in August 642. (Mercia was one of seven Anglo-Saxon kingdoms in Britain, its name derived from the Saxon word 'mierce' meaning 'boundary'.)

Penda led a unified Mercian and Welsh assault against the saint-to-be, which culminated in Oswald's death at the Battle of Maserfield on the north Wales border.

It was said that Penda ritually dismembered Oswald's body, then nailed it to a tree as an offering to the pagan god Woden, thus giving the English border town of Oswestry, or 'Oswald's Tree' its name.

St Oswald's Well
Heritage Green, Winwick
near Warrington, Cheshire
OS Landranger Map No.109:
SJ 607 941

About a mile to the north of the saint's church in a field alongside the A573 road between Winwick and Golborne at Hermitage Green is the holy well on what is believed to have been the exact spot where Oswald was dismembered by King Penda's men

St Oswald's Well,
Heritage Green, Winwick

left: pool beside St Oswald's Well, Winnick

above: statue of St Oswald at his church in Winwick

below: the Hermit public house, conveniently located just across the road from St Oswald's Well in Winwick

St Oswald's Well

Maserfield, Oswestry, Shropshire
OS Explorer Map No.240: SJ 284 294

The story of the dismembered saint continues with the report of an eagle (or sometimes a raven) picking up one of the king's severed arms from the stake at Winwick and flying south. This currently unimpressive and spiritless well is where, according to legend, the bird dropped the limb, and where as a result a miraculous fountain burst forth. From that time onwards, St Oswald's Well developed a powerful reputation for divination and healing, especially for those with eye troubles. Many rites were recommended, including visiting the well at midnight, filling your hands with its waters, then drinking part of it at the same time as forming a wish in your mind. You were then to throw the remainder of the water towards a particular stone at the back of the well, behind which King Oswald's head was thought to have been buried and where a carved, crowned head was set … until its features were entirely worn away by the practice.

Another rite here entailed the search among the nearby trees for an empty beechnut-husk which resembled a human face. Your wish would be granted if this, thrown into the water with the face uppermost, floated on the waters while the petitioner counted to twenty!

St Oswald's Well, Maserfield, Oswestry, at which a "scheme of improvements" was undertaken by Oswestry Town Council in 1985!

above and left: There is little to impress or move today at **St Oswald's Well**, near Holywell in Flintshire, hidden as it is in the side of a bank adjacent to Mertyn Cottage. (OS Explorer Map No.265: 777 168)

HOLY WELLS IN THE AGE OF THE WARRIOR PRINCES

above and far right: The remains of this Anglo-Saxon Minster and later medieval Priory in Gloucester – originally constructed around the year 900 by Aethelflaed, the daughter of King Alfred the Great – was dedicated to the memory of St Oswald and was believed to have once held his relics.

near right: banner of St Oswald from the Church of St Oswald King and Martyr, Oswestry

marching on

In September 1066, Duke William of Normandy landed in Sussex and a month later defeated and killed King Harold II at the Battle of Hastings, setting in train the Norman occupation of Britain … and a further age of Welsh resistance. William's men were formidable warriors descended from Viking settlers, and their conquest brought great changes which would persist for centuries throughout the land, and in particular for the people of the Borderlands of Wales and England.

To reward his warlords for their exertions at Hastings and elsewhere, William 'the Conqueror', now William I of England gave them free rein to use their private armies to carve out their own small kingdoms here, defining in the process a new borderland, the so-called 'Welsh Marches'. He installed three of his most trusted supporters, Hugh d'Avranches, Roger de Montgomerie, and William fitz Osbern as Earls of Chester, Shrewsbury and Hereford, respectively. Among their responsibilities was the containing of the Welsh, an objective which took a century and was never fully achieved in what was to become an often-savage frontier society of small gains and small losses.

HOLY WELLS IN THE AGE OF THE WARRIOR PRINCES

Here, at first, the new Marcher Lords built wooden defensive palisades, often on mounds captured from the Welsh. Many of these were later upgraded to impressive castles of stone at intervals along a line between Chester and Chepstow to nullify the opposition of their western neighbours, and sometimes also the threats of other Marcher Lords.

The powerful barons introduced Anglo-Norman, a northern dialect of Old French – alongside Latin in official documents – threatening the Welsh tongue. They made laws, levied taxes and confiscated land, and often dealt with troublesome elements savagely and without pity. And there were very many troublesome elements. In western Mercia, Eadric the Wild and his Welsh allies led the resistance to the Normans in the second half of the eleventh century, attacking the Norman castle at Hereford in 1067 and later burning down the stronghold at Shrewsbury, before being defeated by William in 1069. Rhys ap Tewdwr, a Prince of Deheubarth in south-west Wales and a descendent of Hywel Dda, was "slain by the Frenchmen who were inhabiting Brycheiniog" in 1093, "and with him fell the kingdom of the Britons" (*Brut y Tywysogion [Chronicle of the Princes]*), despite his earlier accommodations with the Anglo-Norman crown.

opposite: the famous Norman archway at Strata Florida Abbey

right: the graves of Welsh chieftains, their names now forgotten

In 1093, Gruffydd ap Cynan, the King of Gwynedd escaped from a Marcher prison in Chester to join the Welsh anti-Norman rebellion. And Llywelyn ap Iorwerth ('Llywelyn the Great'), Gruffydd ap Cynan's great-grandson; and especially Iorwerth's son Llywelyn ap Gruffydd ('Llywelyn the Last') won significant concessions and offered a temporary and uneasy peace for the Welsh until the latter's death at his last battle in 1282.

But, it is Owain Glyndŵr, a descendant of the princes of Powys who best illustrated this heroic period of Celtic Marcher rebellion, organising a Welsh parliament in Machynlledd in 1402 and establishing himself as the ruler of the whole of Wales.

BORDERLANDS

Llywelyn the Great: a second achilles *

Llywelyn, living man, this is my history lesson,
An instant's shocked discovery
That I am able to claim what is mine,

To fashion with blunt words my own design
Of the cross. All we need is the courage
To look around and we will find our own
Mythology. Here, on native ground.

Robert Minhinnick, from 'The Strata: To Llywelyn Sion'

Llywelyn ap Iorwerth or 'Llywelyn the Great' – the self-styled 'Prince of North – dominated much of Wales for nearly forty years until his death in 1240. He achieved this by a combination of warfare (he fought against his uncles and both of the English Kings John and Henry III, as well as their Anglo-Norman Marcher Lords); diplomacy (making alliances and signing treaties when it suited his purposes); and marriage (Llywelyn himself married King John's albeit-illegitimate daughter Joan in 1205, and arranged a number of diplomatic matches for his own daughters).

Llywelyn's position as Prince was confirmed by King John in the *Magna Carta* signed in 1215, and between 1220 and 1230 he built a series of impressive stone castles at Criccieth, Deganwy, Dolbadarn, Dolwyddelan and Castell y Bere to secure his borders.

In 1238, Llywelyn held a Grand Council of Welsh Princes at Strata Florida Cistercian Abbey, today situated just outside Pontrhydfendigaid, near Tregaron in the county of Ceredigion.

When Edward I invaded Wales, Strata Florida Abbey (established in 1164) was burnt to the ground, to be rebuilt in 1294. And later, after 1401, it became the military base of Henry IV during the early years of the rebellion of Owain Glyndŵr when he punished the monks who had sided with Glyndŵr and plundered the building. Then later, in the 1540s, after Dissolution, the refectory and dormitory were rebuilt as a private house and much of its stonework was recycled within the surrounding buildings.

opposite: The mysterious stone-lined and stepped basin / well in the Monks' Choir at Strata Florida was not re-discovered until the mid twentieth century. Some believe that it may have been used in a rite known as the *mandatum*, when the feet of the brothers were washed by the abbot on the Thursday of Holy Week (Maundy Thursday).

* "the lord Llywelyn ap Iorwerth son of Owain Gwynedd, Prince of Wales, a second Achilles, died having taken on the habit of religion at Aberconwy, and was buried honourably." *Brut y Tywysogion*, 1240

BORDERLANDS

Llywelyn died on 11 April 1240 and was buried at the Cistercian Abbey he had founded at Aberconwy:

True lord of the land – how strange that today
He rules not o'er Gwynedd;
Lord of nought but the piled up stones of his tomb,
Of the seven-foot grave in which he lies.

the poet **Einion Wan**'s lament for Llywelyn the Great

The Prince was succeeded by his son Dafydd ap Llywelyn after Llywelyn amended Welsh law to ensure that, for the very first time, only fully legitimate offspring could inherit (he had had an earlier son, Gruffydd with a woman who was not his wife). But Dafydd died childless in February 1246 and was succeeded by the bastard Gruffydd's two eldest sons Llywelyn and Owain, who divided the country between themselves until Llywelyn ap Gruffydd, known after his death as 'Llywelyn the Last' defeated his unfortunate brother at the battle of Bryn Derwin in 1255.

opposite: the Llywelyn Monument at Cilmeri, near Builth Wells, erected in 1956

Llywelyn the Last: crowned in mockery

The weak and the strong were kept by his hand,
It is every cradled child that screams.

the poet **Gruffudd ab yr Ynad Coch**, writing in 1282, the year of Llywelyn ap Gruffydd's death

Llywelyn ap Gruffydd, the last prince of an independent Wales before its conquest by Edward I of England, was born in 1223. By early 1258, Llywelyn was using the title of Prince of Wales and after a number of impressive military successes ("Ambitious even to Brittany") the designation was recognised by King Henry III in the Treaty of Montgomery in 1267.

Llywelyn dominated Wales for nearly four decades until – following Edward I's succession – his death in December 1282 fighting to push back the borders of the new king and his Marcher Lords at the Battle of Orewin (or Irfon) Bridge at Cilmeri near Builth Wells.

Man who ruled Wales, boldly I'll name him,
Manly Llywelyn, bravest of Welshmen,
Man not enamoured of too easy a way.

the poet **Bleddyn Fardd** (1255-85), from his *Elegy for Llywelyn ap Gruffudd, the Last Prince*

BORDERLANDS

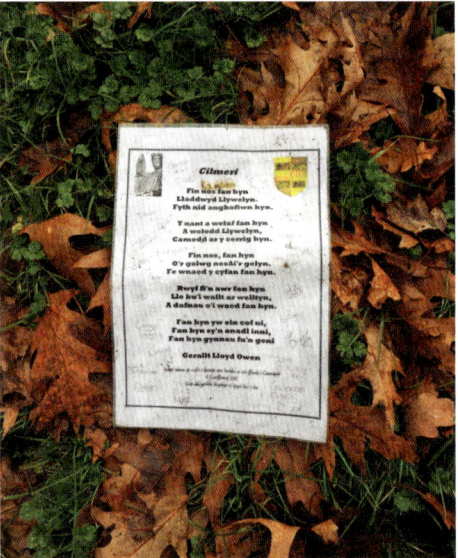

right above: the Llywelyn Monument at Cilmeri, near Builth Wells,
right middle: a poem left at the Llywelyn ap Gruffydd Monument
right below: objects left at the Llywelyn ap Gruffydd Monument
far right: the Victorian Society of Wales at the Llywelyn ap Gruffydd Well on a well-hunting trip led by the author
(OS Explorer Map No.188: SO 001 514)

Llywelyn's head was severed from his body and his corpse was thrown into a roughly-dug grave, from which it is said a spring immediately erupted. Today, at the site, above the well, a giant monolith has been raised – known as Cefn-y-Bedd ('The Ridge of the Grave') – to remember the leader, his hopes for Wales and his last fateful campaign.

Most of Llywelyn's surviving relatives ended their days in captivity, and a contemporary chronicler, writing on the revenge taken on the royal house of Llywelyn ap Gruffydd by King Edward I declared: 'and then all Wales was cast to the ground".

The Norman imperative to verify the defeat of this Welsh champion meant a long journey for Llywelyn's head, first to Edward himself at Rhuddlan, then on to his troops based in Anglesey, and then to London, where it was garlanded with ivy leaves in mockery of the ancient Welsh prophecy that said that a Welshman would one day be crowned in London as king of the whole of Britain.

above right: the cracked stone marker above Llywelyn's Well
right: the Llywelyn Well hidden and revealed

above top: The Cistercian Abbey of Cwm Hir, near Llandrindod Wells, Radnorshire / Powys sat at the bloody crossroads of Welsh history. Some claim that the headless body of Llywelyn ap Gruffudd was brought here for burial after his final battle against the English forces at Irfon Bridge.
opposite and above: memorial slab of Llywelyn ap Gruffydd at Abbey Cwm Hir

HOLY WELLS IN THE AGE OF THE WARRIOR PRINCES

and blood bestains the sun *

Murder and pillage were regularly met by resistance and sometimes savage revenge from the Welsh. The valley of the Dore (or *Dŵr* in Welsh) is said to have run "red with blood for three days" when the Welsh set upon a band of Highlanders resting on its banks after battle, at a place from that time known as Scotland Bank.

On another occasion, in 1175, William de Braose, the so-called 'ogre of all Lord Marchers' and court favourite of King John, invited one Seisyllt ap Dyfnwal, the lord of Castell Arnallt and seventy-four other Welsh princes and chieftains to share a Christmas feast with him at Abergavenny Castle at which they were to resolve a long-standing dispute. The Welsh, convinced by de Braose's assurances, left their weapons outside the banqueting hall … and were all then mercilessly slaughtered, in defiance of the rules of hospitality. De Braose followed this treacherous act with the capture of Sytsyllt's wife, Angharad and the murder of his seven year-old son, Cadwaladr.

Some years later, the Welsh, led by Hywel ap Iorwerth took their revenge on the de Braose knights, although the Marcher Lord himself managed to escape.

above: The elevated site of the hunting lodge 'keep' – built on the motte at Abergavenny Castle in Monmouthshire in the early nineteenth century – has a history that goes back to Bronze and Iron Age settlements, before the Romans (who knew it as *Gobannium*) and, most significantly, the Normans constructed their fortress here in 1075.
In the twelfth century, the castle regularly changed hands between Welsh and English forces. William Camden, the sixteenth century antiquarian claimed that this place "has been oftner stain'd with the infamy of treachery, than any other castle in Wales".

* from the ballad A Walesi Bárdok ('The Bards of Wales'), 1857, by the Hungarian poet János Arany

BORDERLANDS

top: The motte and bailey castle at **Sycharth** in the valley of the River Cynllaith, near Llansilin in Montgomeryshire / Powys was the birthplace and early home of Owain Glyndwr. Situated less than a kilometre from the present English border, this - according to the poet Gryffudd Llwyd ab Einion (c. 1380-1410) – was "a gathering place for battle". (OS Explorer Map No.240: SJ 205 258)

Owain Glyndŵr: not in the roll of common men *

His future, spinning its mythology,
Rides towards him like a prophecy.

Gillian Clarke, from the poem 'Lesson' in *Owain Glyndŵr 1400-2000*

Born in either 1349, 1350, 1354 or 1359 (depending on your sources) and educated in London, Owain Glyndŵr initially fought in the service of the English against the Scots, the Irish and the French.

But being of Welsh aristocratic stock – one of the few living representatives of the old royal houses of Wales whose family had battled alongside Llywelyn ap Gruffydd in the last war of independence – Glyndŵr was destined for greater things.

In the words of Gwyn A Williams, he "fulfilled many of the mystical medieval prophecies about the rising up of the red dragon". (*Wales: The Rough Guide*, 1994)

* from William Shakespeare's description of Owain Glyndwr in *Henry IV, Part I*

HOLY WELLS IN THE AGE OF THE WARRIOR PRINCES

opposite below and below: It was at his mound at **Glyndyfrdwy**, overlooking the valley of the river Dee near Llangollen that Glyndwr proclaimed himself Prince of Wales on 16 September 1400, so beginning his fourteen-year rebellion against English rule. (OS Explorer Map No.256: SJ 126 431)

BORDERLANDS

Although roused to action in the first instance by a simple border dispute with his neighbour over land rights, Owain Glyndŵr's and Wales' grievances went much deeper. After Edward I had defeated much of Wales in 1282, the Norman king set about populating the border towns with English settlers, administered, often harshly, by his Marcher Lords. Heavy taxes, discriminatory laws against the native population and exclusive rights and privileges for the incomers created a medieval system of apartheid and, by 1400, the Welsh had become second-class citizens in their own land. So, it was no surprise that, when Owain raised his standard in Ruthin on 16 September 1400, passionate supporters appeared from all parts of the country … and he was proclaimed the Prince of Wales. And, equally predictably, in quick response, the English Parliament intensified its anti-Welsh legislation and Henry IV marched his army into Wales to quell the rebellion of these Welsh "rascals", these "bare-footed clowns".

The next four years saw a series of military successes for Glyndŵr against all the odds. In 1402, his troops defeated a large English force led by Henry Percy ('Hotspur') at the battle of Shrewsbury; and then that of Edmund Mortimer, the young Earl of March, at the Battle of Bryn Glas, at Pilleth near Presteigne, at one of the most significant moments in the Welsh War of Independence.

HOLY WELLS IN THE AGE OF THE WARRIOR PRINCES

St Mary's Well
Pilleth, near Knighton,
Radnorshire / Powys
OS Explorer map No.201: SO 256 683

….. his dream becomes a deed,
when an old idea takes up its sword to wake
an imagined nation from sleep.

Gillian Clarke, from the poem 'Ruthin Market' in *Owain Glyndŵr 1400 – 2000*

Pilleth is a small village two miles south of Knighton in Radnorshire / Powys. It is the site of an ancient church and a holy well, now dedicated to St Mary, both of which stand on Bryn Glas Hill overlooking the valley of the River Lugg.

It was here that Owain Glyndŵr recorded one of his most important early successes in his struggle against the English. Significantly, this was the site where legend claimed that the Briton Caradog (Caractacus) had made his last stand against a previous invasion, that of a Roman army led by Publius Ostorius Scapula some thirteen centuries before, a belief which would have added fire to the bellies of the Welsh.

And so it was that on St Alban's Day (22 June 1402), Glyndŵr defeated an army led by Sir Edmund Mortimer.

Despite having a much smaller force, Glyndŵr prevailed at Pilleth through the employment of superior tactics and the skills of the Welsh longbow-men.

It was claimed that, immediately after the battle, the English corpses were mutilated by Welsh women seeking revenge for King Henry IV's many acts of brutality against them, although this assertion is questioned by some historians who see the account as a slander perpetrated by the English parliament to portray the Welsh as savages, and legitimise their suppression.

Mortimer who was captured during the battle quickly renounced his allegiance to Henry, married Caitrin, the Welsh Prince's daughter, and added his forces to those of Owain Glyndŵr.

There are various explanations for the origin of the name, Pilleth. One intriguingly suggests it came from Pwll-y Llethr (Welsh for 'The Pit on the Slope'), which could refer to the healing well found today to the north of the tower in the church cemetery. It was said that Glyndŵr's soldiers quenched their thirst, here, both before and after their victory.

opposite: well painting, St Mary's Church, Pilleth
top: St Mary's Church and graveyard
left: St Mary's Holy Well, St Mary's Church

167

Henry IV's third expedition into Wales in August 1402 was defeated by the elements, the torrential rain adding to Owain's legendary status as the belief soon circulated that he could even control the weather, although RS Thomas was sure that: "Nothing that Glyn Dwr / Knew was armour against the rain's / Missiles". ('A Welsh Testament', 1961)

By the end of 1403, as Glyndŵr took castle after castle and Henry's troops failed to arrest his progress, the Prince controlled most of Wales. In response, the English king enacted more punishing laws against the Welsh, including prohibiting the practices of Welsh-language bards and singers. In 1404, at the high point of the rebellion, Glyndŵr assembled a parliament at Machynlleth and was crowned king of a free Wales in the presence of leaders from Scotland, France and Spain.

A second sitting in Harlech a year later saw Glyndŵr making plans to divide England and Wales into three parts between Mortimer, Thomas Percy the earl of Northumberland, and himself.

But Owain's vision of a new free Wales went far beyond the territorial; he had dreams for two universities, Welsh-speaking bishops and the recognition of St David's as a major ecclesiastical centre.

Although Glyndŵr's struggle continued for the next six years or more, it never fulfilled its promise to free Wales from the Anglo-Norman yoke. One by one, his castles began to fall to the forces of the king, and Glyndŵr's own family was captured, and his brother killed. The Prince took to the woods, a fugitive refusing the pardon offered him by the king in return for his submission, and continued to conduct his bloody, though finally fruitless guerrilla campaign against the old enemy.

Glyndŵr was never captured, however, and the story of his last days are uncertain. Some say he was cared for by his daughter at Monnington Court on the banks of the Wye in Herefordshire, and died and was buried there in an unmarked grave in 1416. Others claim his last resting place was Kentchurch Court, the home of the Scudamore family, but no one really knows, keeping alive the powerful symbolism of an ageing warrior who, like Arthur, could not die and will come again to lead his people in future times of trouble.

Somewhere in our darkest history
the body of a sleeping king lies low
under the earth, under unknown trees
of the border forests …

From the grave, below the unmarked stones,
six hundred years of myth grow from his bones.

Gillian Clarke, from the poem 'The Sleeping King' in *Owain Glyndŵr 1400-2000*

After Owain, the anti-Welsh laws remained on the statute books until the mixed blessing in 1485 of the accession to the English throne of Henry VII (1457-1509). The new king claimed to be descended from a daughter of Llywelyn the Great, giving the Welsh an expectation of a new kind of relationship with its eastern neighbours. This was a false hope, however, and Wales soon became fully subsumed within the English state, with its leadership largely accepting Anglicisation:

"Tudor enthusiasts among Welsh historians delighted in portraying Henry VII's court as a place where the Welsh were held in high regard, but there was little advantage in the king vaunting his Welsh connections in London, where love of things Welsh was hardly rampant.

By descent, Henry VII was a quarter Welsh, a quarter French and half English, and it was his English blood that gave him a claim to the throne of England."

Dr John Davies
from *Wales under the Tudors*, 2011

HOLY WELLS IN THE AGE OF THE WARRIOR PRINCES

In 1489, Ludlow, the engine house of the Marcher Lords' power, became the seat of the 'Council of the King in the Dominion and Principality of Wales and the Marches', and Tudor rule while restricting Marcher authority added power to the monarch.

In February 1536, the English parliament (with no Welsh representatives present) approved 'Act 27 Hen.VII xxvi – clause 26 of the acts passed in the 27th year of the reign of Henry VII', later to be known as the 'Act of Union' when Wales became:

Although Edmund Burke wrote confidently in 1780 that "As from that moment, as by a charm, the tumults subsided….peace, order and civilization followed in the train of liberty", this Act of annexation meant that now, in the eyes of the law, the Welsh were English.

"incorporated, annexed, united and subiecte to and under the imperialle Crown of this Realme as a very member…of the same."

Ludlow Castle from Whitcliffe Common hill

BORDERLANDS

Fortresses of the Borderlands: the very perfection of decay *

One of the most, perhaps the most important consideration for the location of a defensive castle – along with its elevation and outlook – is the presence of water.

Evidence of the millennia of fortress building along the shifting Wales / England border – be it that of the earliest settlers, or of the Roman outposts built to control the native tribes, or those of later Saxon invaders, or the Norman citadels of the Marcher Lords, or Llywelyn ap Iorwerth's thirteenth century castles in the north and west, or of Owain Glyndŵr's fifteenth century mounds at the sites of the last real military battles for Welsh independence – the siting of all of these is predicated upon finding a substantial and reliable source of clean drinking water.

* Daniel Defoe, describing Ludlow Castle in 1722

Bronllys Castle

near Talgarth, Breconshire / Powys
OS Outdoor Leisure Map No.13:
SO 149 347

The Norman lord, Richard fitz Pons built a timber motte and bailey castle on this site in the eleventh century to hold land captured from the Welsh. By 1165, it had been reinforced with stone, then fully re-modelled in around 1230 by William de Clifford III to the structure we see today. William, it seems, understood well the nature of Borderland politics, being a Marcher Lord by the authority of Henry III of England at the same time as the husband of Margaret, the daughter of Llywelyn ab Iorwerth, Prince of Gwynedd.

During Owain Glyndŵr's uprising, he attacked and caused substantial damage to the Bronllys structure, in both 1400 and 1409.

opposite: the Raglan Castle well
in the Pitched Stone Court

right: Bronllys Castle,
near Talgarth

BORDERLANDS

left above: Bronllys Castle

left middle, below and opposite: The Bronllys Castle well is situated a little way away from the main tower in the place where the Grand Hall once stood.

BORDERLANDS

Beeston Castle

Beeston Castle, Tarporley, Cheshire
OS Landranger Map No.117:
SJ 539 593

The evocative ruins of the thirteenth century Beeston Castle – begun in 1226 by Ranulf de Blondeville, the sixth earl of Chester (1170-1232) – standing high upon a rocky crag above the Cheshire Plain were first used as a fortress in the Bronze Age.

When the castle passed to the crown after the death of Ranulf's son in 1237, Henry III used Beeston as a garrison fort and a prison during his wars in Wales, affording as the elevation does spectacular views over the contested Borderlands. A century after Henry, its natural defences were further strengthened by Edward II.

There are two wells at Beeston, one in the outer and one in the inner ward, the later of much greater importance at times of siege, as between 1644 and 1645 during the English Civil War. There is a legend that into this inner well – which is believed to be 370 feet deep – Richard II threw a treasure of "100,000 marks in gold coin and 100,000 marks in other precious objects", before embarking upon a trip to Ireland in 1399.

above left: the entance to the inner castle at Beeston, Tarporley, Cheshire
below left: the view over the Cheshire Plain from Beeston Castle
above right: the inner ward well at Beeston

opposite: the now-dry outer ward well at Beeston Castle

Ludlow Castle

Castle Square, Ludlow, Shropshire
OS Explorer Map No.203: SO 508 745

Construction of the castle at Ludlow – with its steep defensive slopes to north and west above the natural barriers of the rivers Teme and Corve – began in the late eleventh century as a Border stronghold of the Marcher Lord, Roger de Lacy. It was here in 1224 that the rebel prince, Llywelyn ap Iorwerth signed a peace treaty with Henry III.

The castle was enlarged and made more comfortable domestically by its next tenant, Peter de Geneville in the latter part of the thirteenth century, after Edward I's harsh Welsh campaign had brought more stable conditions to the border.

right and above: the unusual twelfth century Round Chapel dedicated to Mary Magdelene at Ludlow Castle (exterior and interior)

HOLY WELLS IN THE AGE OF THE WARRIOR PRINCES

Ludlow Castle, Shropshire
from the bridge over the river Teme

BORDERLANDS

In 1474, the castle was established as the seat of the Council of the Marches of Wales, the main Borderland court where laws were passed and criminal, ecclesiastical and civil cases heard. This made Ludlow effectively the capital of Wales, a situation which regularly attracted the anger and military response of the disenfranchised Celts.

The Council's authority was greatly extended after 1534 when Bishop Rowland Lee was appointed as Lord President. It was reported that he enforced the law unsparingly so that "all the thieves in Wales quaked for feare".

Extracts from the Council's records include the following:

wales is far out of order and there have been many murders in Oswestery and Powys (1533)

the scarcines of grain arises daily and it causes more roberies (1534)

And in 1579, its papers reported that two men had been appointed "to test the propties of the water at Saint Winifreds well in Flintshire and destroy well if not medicinal".

The Council was finally abolished – after more than 200 years – in July 1689, and the control of England and Wales centralised in London. The castle after this date soon crumbled to a ruin.

above: images of Ludlow Castle well, sited in the Great Tower Court in the inner bailey, the most impregnable part of the fortress

Stokesay Castle
near Craven Arms, Shropshire
OS Explorer Map No.217: SO 437 817

I have rarely had ... the sensation of dropping back personally into the past so straight as while I lay on the grass beside the well in the little sunny court of this small castle and lazily appreciated the still definite details of mediaeval life.

Henry James (1843-1916), writing about Stokesay in *Cathedrals and Castles*, 1905

Built in the late thirteenth century on profits from the trade in fine Welsh wool, Stokesay Castle in the valley of the river Onny near Craven Arms is one of the finest medieval fortified manor houses in Britain, although its military appearance and now-dry defensive moat were largely decorative. Stokesay illustrates "the peaceful side of the Middle Ages" (*Stokesay Castle guidebook, English Heritage*) at a once-luxurious site which suffered little from the bloody conflict common at most other Borderland castles.

HOLY WELLS IN THE AGE OF THE WARRIOR PRINCES

Stokesay Castle

BORDERLANDS

This was for most of its history a place of commerce and of culture. It was reported that when Isabel Ludlow, the lady of the house, gave birth in 1424, William her proud husband paid three shillings and four pence to three minstrels to celebrate the occasion with music, a sum not quite equalled two and a half centuries later when the then owner, Charles Baldwyn paid two shillings to the bell ringers of the local church "for ringing at the birth of the lord's son".

above: Stokesay Castle's ornate seventeenth century gatehouse and well, the latter's position outside of the main fortified building confirming the Castle's peaceful past
left: a room in the thirteenth century south tower, Stokesay

HOLY WELLS IN THE AGE OF THE WARRIOR PRINCES

Raglan Castle
Raglan, Monmouthshire
OS Explorer Map OL14: SO 415 084

[its] hundred rooms filled with festive fare,
its hundred chimneys for men of high degree

Dafydd Llwyd ap Llywelyn ap Gruffudd (c.1400 - c.1490), the poet, writing about Raglan Castle

Although its foundations probably go back to the time of the Norman invasion of Gwent in the late eleventh century, the inspiring castle building we see at Raglan today was begun in 1435 by Sir William ap Thomas, the fifth son of a minor Welsh gentry family who was later to be honoured by Henry VI as 'the blue knight of Gwent'.

Significantly added to by William's son, Baron Herbert (who, as a major supporter of the House of York, was to become the most powerful Welshman of his day), and after him by the Bloet family, it was the Somersets (Earls of Worcester) who made the last sumptuous additions to the castle, including its fine Renaissance gardens, complete with marble statues of Roman emperors.

Henry Tudor spent his childhood at Raglan, and Charles I had on many occasions been entertained here. During the English Civil War (1642-1651), the castle strengthened its defences and held out for the king against the New Model Army until it eventually fell during the siege of 1646.

The castle was damaged by the bombardment and the victorious parliamentary forces set about demolishing the palace-fortress, stripping the lead from the roofs, destroying the forests and the water gardens, and burning the library which housed one of the finest collection of Welsh manuscripts and books in the land. And, in later centuries, like so many other tumbled ruins, it was used as a cheap and easy source of building materials for new constructions.

At the height of its opulence, Raglan Castle was graced with two fine wells – one in the Great Tower (the most secure area) and one in the Pitched Stone Court – as well as an ornamental marble fountain known as 'The White Horse' in the aptly-titled Fountain Court, and another in the moat. In 1663, Edward Somerset wrote a book about great inventions, one of which was the 'water commanding machine' he himself had designed which it was claimed could spout water from the Raglan moat as high as the top of the Great Tower.

top and middle: all that remains of "The Fountaine trim, that runs both day and night" (Thomas Churchyard from his poem, 'The Worthines of Wales', 1587)
below: Raglan outer well

BORDERLANDS

left: Raglan Castle gatehouse from above

left and below: the Raglan Castle well in the Great Tower

the ancient wrong

The Principality of Wales existed between the years 1216 with Llywelyn ap Iorwerth's rule over what was then the whole of Wales, and 1543 when England and Wales were formally merged through the Laws in Wales Acts. Since that latter date, the title of the Prince of Wales – automatically granted now to the heir apparent to the reigning monarch of the United Kingdom of Great Britain and Northern Ireland – has had no constitutional role or formal responsibilities within the land.

In one of his finest poems, **AE Housman** (1859-1936) explores the abiding and bloody history of Borderland tensions in the landscape where he lived, made the more resonant by the fact that his mother was Welsh and his father from Lancaster in England:

The Welsh Marches

High the vanes of Shrewsbury gleam
Islanded in Severn stream;
The bridges from the steepled crest
Cross the water east and west.

The flag of morn in conqueror's state
Enters at the English gate:
The vanquished eve, as night prevails,
Bleeds upon the road to Wales.

Ages since the vanquished bled
Round my mother's marriage-bed;
There the ravens feasted far
About the open house of war:

When Severn down to Buildwas ran
Coloured with the death of man,
Couched upon her brother's grave
The Saxon got me on the slave.

The sound of fight is silent long
That began the ancient wrong;
Long the voice of tears is still
That wept of old the endless ill.

In my heart it has not died,
The war that sleeps on Severn side;
They cease not fighting, east and west,
On the marches of my breast.

Here the truceless armies yet
Trample, rolled in blood and sweat;
They kill and kill and never die;
And I think that each is I.

None will part us, none undo
The knot that makes one flesh of two,
Sick with hatred, sick with pain,
Strangling – When shall we be slain?

When shall I be dead and rid
Of the wrong my father did?
How long, how long, till spade and hearse
Put to sleep my mother's curse?

(*A Shropshire Lad*, XXVIII, 1896)

* WHEN PALLID CHEEKS REGAIN THEIR ROSEATE BLUSH
a new fashion for spas

above: bathtub, Pump Rooms
Tenbury Spa, Worcestershire

Nay! Foreigners of rank who look this o'er
To try the Wells may quit their native shore;
For when they learn the virtues of this spaw
Twice tens of thousands to the spot 'twill draw;
As when its wond'rous powers are pointed out
And men found cap'ring who have had the Gout;
When pallid cheeks regain their roseate blush *
And vig'rous health expels the hectic flush;
When those once hypp'd appear quite blythe and gay,
And those once crippl'd cast the crutch away;
Sure when the pride of British Spas they see
They'll own the humble instrument in me!

from an English spa guidebook of 1808

below: Trefriw Spa elbow bath and weighing scales with notice that reads: To WEIGH oneself OFTEN / Is to KNOW oneself WELL / To known oneself WELL / Is to BE WELL

The prospects for Borderland wells improved dramatically in the late eighteenth century when a new 'scientific' recognition of the beneficial properties of natural springs exploded into the craze for medicinal spas, giving the fortunate towns where they appeared a huge new lease of life. Signifying the presence of a mineral spring, the word 'spa' comes from the town of Spa in Belgium, where its residents claimed that drinking its iron-bearing waters had from medieval times cured a variety of illnesses.

The popularity of this new/old practice of 'taking the waters' saw those rich enough flocking in their thousands to Llandrindod, Trefriw, Llanwrtyd, Builth, Cheltenham, Tenbury, Droitwich, the Malvern towns and elsewhere to drink from and immerse themselves within their saline, sulphur, iodine, alum, magnesium, barium chloride and chalybeate basins and pools.

Glowing accounts of the medical successes of these places were common. A 1774 Llandrindod journal reported:

"A man who lives near the spring… told me he was ill for several years and so windy and costive that his life was a burden to him. He appealed to several apothecaries and physicians who gave him no relief. He at last took to the waters of which he drunk 23 pints which brought from him an excrement so hard as could make little of no impression on when stamped with the heel of a shoe! This man is upwards of 70 years old and has drank the water frequently after and hath never had a sick day since that time and looks though grey the healthiest man I have seen of his age."

This was, in reality, a time of the re-discovery of the benefits of the bath house and of thermal bathing, first introduced to the area by the Romans. Alongside the blossoming of a renewed interest in classical architecture and culture, it is not surprising that many of the 'new' spas surfaced at sites where much older bathers had sought relief and communion in the past. From the earlier admonitions of the church to refrain from seeking either spiritual solace or physical pleasure in water, visiting a British spa during the 'season' now became the height of good taste and sophistication, as much a place to be seen as to be cured.

But hydropathy treatments were often extreme and full of discomforts, as terrifying in some cases as the custom known as 'bowsening', inflicted upon the mentally-disturbed in much earlier days when the unfortunate was pushed backwards into a sacred pool, a practice repeated until the demons fled the demented!

Included in the later spa towns' 'punishments' were 'wet sheeting', where a patient was wrapped like a mummy in soaking linen sheets; and the 'douche', where stinging, ice-cold water was showered over the naked cure-seeker from above, below or, in some cases, from all sides, which one eighteenth-century patient aptly termed "a good rehearsal for Purgatory".

And of the 'lamp bath', another who experienced that torture wrote: "There is nothing so likely to draw the gravy out of a man … it is for all the world like being a fat goose before a slow fire"!

the healthiest place in Wales *

Trefriw Spa
Trefriw, near Betws-y-Coed, Conwy
OS Landranger Map No. 115:
SH 780 652

Trefriw is situated on the western slopes of the Conwy valley, just a few miles south of the Roman fort of *Canovium*, and beside Sarn Helen, the major Roman road which ran from this military settlement to another at Tomen-y-mur and on to *Moridunum* at present-day Carmarthen. Not surprisingly, then, the copious spring at Trefriw was recognised and used by the Romans many centuries before its chalybeate and sulphur-rich waters were developed into one of the country's most important spa destinations in the early eighteen hundreds.

Trefriw's popularity grew throughout the nineteenth and into the first half of the twentieth century with its well-healed visitors arriving by steamer from Conwy and by train. It is interesting to note that Trefriw's first passenger boat, introduced in 1847, was called St Winifred (see Chapter 3, *Holy Wells in the Age of the Saints*).

At its height in the early years of the twentieth century, six steamers a day were carrying more than one thousand visitors on the ninety-minute journey to its pump rooms, bath houses, tea shops, restaurants and hotels.

One explanation for the origin of the name of the village is *'tref'* (farmsted, or alternatively town) and *'briw'* (a wound), refering to the ability of the waters here to heal, a claim supported by many, not least local woman Mary Owen 'The Oldest Subject in Great Britain' who died in 1911 at the age of 108!

Those seeking cures were further enticed by Trefriw Spa's five-star reviews: "inconceivably nasty and correspondingly efficacious" (in *Baddeley's Thorough Guide to North Wales*, 1895) and "probably the best spa in the United Kingdom" (from the eminent Dr Hayward, from Liverpool).

Today, the steamers and most of the visitors have gone, but the medicinal waters still flow and are still in great demand. A thriving business, *Spatone*, is based here, packaging and distributing their *Iron+* products internationally, continuing the practice of the Victorian period when a two-month's supply shipped anywhere in the world cost the very considerable sum of forty-two shillings.

above: one of the wooden signs saved from the heyday of the spa industry at Trefriw
below: a slate bath from the old spa bath house

A NEW FASHION FOR SPAS

the salt of life
Droitwich Spa
Droitwich, Worcestershire

Salt extraction in this area dates back to prehistoric times when the local *Cornovii* people boiled the abundant brine which sprang naturally at sites along the Salwarpe river. Elaborate processes were used to produce the salt crystals, so essential in the seasoning and preserving of food, and in the dying of cloth and the production of pottery.

The massive deposits here – laid down some 200 million years ago – were said to contain two and a half pounds (about one kilogramme) of salt per single gallon of brine, ten times more dense than sea water and only rivalled by the Dead Sea. When the Romans arrived, they took over the already-existing trade and named the settlement Salinae (or saltworks).

opposite: the ferrous stalactites in the Roman well at Trefriw

right: a 'Roman' at Droitwich Spa

189

Records show that soldiers at this time were paid partly in salt, which gave rise to the word 'salary'.

Salt making in the 'wiches' of Droitwich, Nantwich, Middlewich, Northwich and elsewhere is mentioned in the Doomsday Book, commissioned by William the Conqueror in 1085 to assess taxation values.

By the late medieval period, it was estimated that more than 1,500 tons of salt were produced annually in Droitwich alone, increasing to 120,000 (one third of the total production in England) by the end of the nineteenth century.

Initially extracted with buckets lowered into deep pits, in later years bore-holes were sunk, opening up the trade to small families of entrepreneurs who operated from their own private dwellings, the so-called 'wich houses', in often difficult and dangerous conditions:

Men toiled long hours, each day, the crust to win
With anxious eyes watched seething, boiling brine
With savage strength resolved the strains within
And cursed the lowly station of their kind

Later, Droitwich's salt springs provided a further boost to the town's fame and fortune … as a spa. But here the waters were not 'taken' as was common elsewhere; instead, muscular pains and diseases were relieved by floating on and swimming in its concentrated warm salt solution. The town's first brine baths were opened in the 1830s, as typhoid and Asiatic cholera epidemics spread across the country. Particularly popular for their thermal properties – being second only to Bath Spa in the whole of Britain in terms of temperature – the efficacy of brine baths to cure these deadly scourges quickly spread.

The last of Droitwich's salt works closed in 1922, and the only operational brine well in the town – on Tower Hill – continued to service the bathing pool at Droitwich Spa private hospital until 'health and safety issues' ended its days in December 2008.

far left: Saltworkers sculpture by John McKenna (1998) in Droitwich town centre
left: a fine reconstruction of the original **Upwich Brine Pit salt mine** (OS Explorer Map No.204: SO 896 637), on the banks of the River Salwarpe, Droitwich

opposite: **Droitwich Spa Lido** (OS Explorer Map No.204: SO 887 632) re-opened to the public in 2007 after its closure in the late 1990s

BORDERLANDS

above and above right: a neglected brine spring
(OS Explorer Map No.257: SJ 649 518)
on the banks of the river Weaver in Nantwich, Cheshire
below right: the sad remains of 'Old Biot',
the ancient brine pit (OS Explorer Map No.257:
SJ 649 526), which now supplies the town's brine
swimming pool

A NEW FASHION FOR SPAS

above: salt working display, Northwich Museum

The first recorded union for salt workers was the Brine Boilers Association, founded in 1845. This trade union banner of 1893 is displayed at the most impressive Northwich Museum.

BORDERLANDS

above left: Led by Cheshire West and Chester Council, and financed by the Heritage Lottery Fund and *manage +*, a new £8million project is currently being undertaken by Wates Construction to restore the Lion Salt Works (OS Explorer Map No.267: SJ 671 755) in the village of Marston just outside Northwich, as a major heritage destination, with an expected opening in spring 2014.
left: The Salt Barge Inn, Marston, near Northwich

opposite: entrance to Rock Park, Llandrindod Wells, framing the Gwalia Hotel

the queen of the well towns of Wales

Llandrindod Wells
Radnorshire / Powys

Here were accommodation for the invalid of whatever rank and distinction, field amusements for the healthy ... balls, billiards and regular assemblies varied the pastimes of the gay and the fashionable.

William Grovesnor, writing about Llandrindod Hall Hotel in 1749

The three kinds of springs – iron, sulphur and saline – found at what we now know as Llandrindod Wells are said by some to have their origins in Celtic mythology.

The story is told of an ancient hero who saves a maiden's life by literally 'liquidising' the three devils that were pursuing her, with the aid of iron, brimstone and salt.

A NEW FASHION FOR SPAS

Although Llandrindod was to become the premier spa town in Wales in the mid-nineteenth century – even considered by some to offer serious competition to the grand English resort of Bath – it seems likely that the curative properties of the mineral waters here were much earlier known and appreciated by the Romans who occupied the Castell Collen military site, one mile north-west of the present town. (see Chapter 2, *The Fine Art of Bathing in Roman Britain*)

The first reliable record for 'taking the waters' at the chalybeate spring in Llandrindod was as early 1696, when the Vaughans of Herefordshire were said to have stayed here for three weeks. The saline and sulphur springs were (re-)discovered in 1732 by a Mrs Jenkins, the tenant of Lower Bach-y-Graig farm. She sold the water to travellers and the fame of its healing properties soon spread. The farm became known as the Pump House, and later was developed as the celebrated Pump House Hotel.

In 1754, a German physician and spa expert who suffered from a variety of diseases visited Llandrindod, drank from its saline and sulphuric springs and was cured. His encouraging comments on the medicinal qualities of the waters set in train the international recognition of Llandrindod as a major spa town:

Their good effects are so conspicuous that they give place to none in Europe ... as yet I have not met with any of the same kind that surpass these at Llandrindod.

Dr DW Linden, from his *Treatise on the Medicinal Waters of Llandrindod*, 1756

The popularity of the Llandrindod waters during the eighteenth century was short-lived, however, as the town's remoteness and its new attractiveness to gamblers and drinkers led to an early decline, not to be halted until the mid-nineteenth century with the advent of the Central Wales Railway line.

Arriving from Knighton in 1865, and eventually connecting with Shrewsbury in one direction and Swansea in the other in 1868, the town was now within easy reach of the urban centres of the north-west, the Midlands and south Wales.

At its height, more than thirty mineral springs, two assembly rooms, a pump room, an ornamental lake, hotels, public houses, tea rooms, churches, shops and everything else needed by the traveller in search of a watery cure sprang up to cater for as many as 90,000 mostly-wealthy visitors each year, as the mid Wales town was transformed into a prosperous and fashionable spa resort:

"there were six attendants in white coats, three each side, serving the various waters. Some days the queue would be nearly up to the park entrance. On one Bank Holiday morning, over 1,000 glasses of water were sold before 9.00 a.m. Some people bought weekly tickets and waters were also delivered daily to the hotels and boarding houses in one or two-gallon jars."

Consumption of between sixteen and eighteen pints a day was normal, and such were the purging qualities of the waters here that one man was reported to have discharged a worm seven feet long and the two inches wide after imbibing.

A NEW FASHION FOR SPAS

BATHS.

EVERY FORM OF SPA TREATMENT FOR RHEUMATISM, SCIATICA, GOUT, NEURITIS, COLITIS, AND SKIN DISEASES.

HIGH STREET SULPHUR & ELECTRICAL BATHS.

THESE BATHS installed in 1909, have been fitted up with the most modern and scientific apparatus, and are now admitted to be equal to any in England or on the Continent.

No Expense has been spared in bringing the Establishment up to this high state of efficiency.

Tea Rooms, Cooling Rooms, Lounges, Electrical Elevator, and all the practical details of Lighting, Heating and Ventilating have been carefully carried out, and everything done for the comfort and convenience of the Patients.

The STRONG NATURAL SULPHUR WATER is obtained from Springs on the Company's Premises, and is pumped direct from the sealed reservoir.

TERMS.

	s.	d.		s.	d.
1 Sulphur Needle Spray, per ten minutes	2	6	21 Tyrnauer Electrical Hot Air Treatment, two limbs, spine, or whole body	7	6
2 Ditto, series of six	12	6	25 Ditto, course of six	40	0
3 Ærated Pine Bath (Prana Sparkling System)	5	0	26 Local Mud Pack, per application	4	0
4 Ditto, series of three	13	0	27 Ditto, Peat Pack, per application	4	0
5 Sitz Bath	3	0	28 **Combined Plombières and Tivoli Treatment**	6	0
6 Liver Pack and Needle Spray	4	0	29 Ditto, series of three	15	0
7 Ditto, series of three	11	0	Plombières Douche, without Tivoli	3	6
8 **Sulphur Aix Douche and Massage**	5	0	30 Hydro Electric Medicated Baths—single ticket	4	0
9 Ditto, series of three	14	0	31 Ditto, ten tickets	11	0
10 **Sulphur Vichy Douche and Massage**	5	0	32 X-Ray Examination	2	6
11 Ditto, series of three	14	0	33 X-Ray Radiograph 12/6 and	21	0
12 **Scotch Douche**, per ten minutes	3	0	34 Medico-Mechanical Treatment	2	6
13 Dry Massage after any treatment, ½ hour, 3/-; ¾ hour, 4/6; 1 hour	7	6	35 Ditto, ten tickets	20	0
			36 Ditto, twenty tickets	35	0
14 Electric Light Bath followed by Pine Bath	6	0	37 Nauheim Bath	5	0
15 Ditto, series of three	15	0	38 Ditto, series of three	13	0
16 Radiant Heat and Arc combined	10	6	39 Chiropody, from	2	6
17 Ditto, series of three	25	0	40 Electrical Massage	5	0
18 Arc Projector, one application	5	0	41 Ditto, course of three	13	0
19 Ditto, three applications	12	6	42 **Vibratory Massage**	4	0
20 Leucodescent Treatment	5	0	43 Ditto, course of six	20	0
21 Ditto, three applications	12	6	44 **Galvanic and Faradic Current Cataphoresis, Ionization**	6	0
22 Tyrnauer Electrical Hot Air Treatment, one limb	5	0	45 Ditto, course of three	15	0
23 Ditto, course of six	27	0	76 X-Ray Treatment, terms on application. 77 Cautery		

Baths and Treatments must be booked by appointment at the Offices either at High Street or Rock Park, and should be paid for at the time of booking.
Both establishments are connected by Private Telephone, also with the Post Office Exchange. Baths may be cancelled on giving two hours' clear notice and returning the Tickets.
A number of these Baths are only given on Medical advice, Patients will prevent delay by producing prescription at time of booking.
To facilitate Treatment, Patients are requested TO ATTEND TEN MINUTES before appointed time. IF A PATIENT IS LATE THE TREATMENT MUST BE CURTAILED.
The Bathing Establishments are open till 6 p.m. Weekdays and 1 p.m. Sundays.
It is expected Patients will not occupy dressing-rooms longer than 15 minutes after a bath. Waiting rooms are provided for the use of Patients after leaving the dressing-rooms.

ROCK PARK BATHS.

(Strong Natural Sulphur Baths).

THE BATHING ESTABLISHMENT adjoins the Rock Park Pump Room, and the Baths are supplied from a new reservoir capable of holding 120,000 gallons of Sulphur Water. This arrangement permits of an ample supply of Natural Water, without in any way interfering with the supply in the Pump Room. The Sulphur Water is pumped into the sealed tank continuously by water power, and as the tank is on high ground overlooking the Baths a good pressure is obtained. This is a matter of vital importance for Needle Sprays, Douches, etc. During the Winter, 1911–1912, the installation and accommodation have been been greatly increased and improved.

TERMS.

	s.	d.		s.	d.
46 Reclining Hot Sulphur Bath, per ten minutes	2	6	62 Ærated Sulphur Bath (Prana System)	5	0
47 Ditto, series of six	12	6	63 Ditto, series of six	25	0
48 Hot Sulphur Douche	2	6	64 Ærated Pine Bath	5	0
49 Ditto, series of six	12	6	65 Ditto, series of six	25	0
50 Sulphur Needle Douche, per ten minutes	2	6	66 Massage, ¼ hour, 3/-; ½ hour, 4/6; 1 hour	7	6
51 Ditto, series of six	12	6	67 Spinal Douche, per ten minutes	3	0
52 Nauheim Bath	5	0	68 Reclining Sulphur Bath with Douche or Spray	3	6
53 Ditto, series of six	25	0			
54 **Circular Needle Spray**, per ten minutes	2	6	69 Ditto, course of six	20	0
55 Ditto, series of six	12	6	70 Needle Spray with Douche or Spray	3	6
56 Sitz Bath	2	6	71 Ditto, course of six	20	0
57 Ditto, series of six	12	6	72 **Sulphur Aix Douche** and Massage	5	0
58 Liver Pack and Needle Spray	4	0	73 Ditto, course of three	14	0
59 Ditto, series of six	21	0	74 **Sulphur Vichy Douche** and Massage	5	0
60 Local Mud Pack, per application	4	0	75 Ditto, course of three	14	0
61 Local Peat Pack, per application	4	0			

The Medical Profession are at all times welcome to inspect the Establishments, and may have a course of Baths (not exceeding three) on presentation of card.

The Establishment does not accept Boarders, Patients will find splendid Hotel and Boarding House accommodation in Llandrindod Wells.

---

opposite left: In 1983, water from this Eye Well in Rock Park, Llandrindod Wells (OS Explorer Map No.200: SO 055 608) was sent to the then-Prime Minister Margaret Thatcher. There is no evidence that it improved her view of Wales or the world.

opposite right: Bath chair (courtesy of Radnorshire Museum, Llandrindod Wells)

left: Spa treatments and charges at Llandrindod Wells, 1911 (courtesy of Radnorshire Museum)

right: the Chalybeate Well (OS Explorer Map No.200: SO 055 608), Rock Park, Llandrindod Wells: The word 'chalybeate' derives from the Chalybes, mythical creatures which inhabited Mount Ida in northern Asia Minor and were said to have invented iron-working.

opposite: the still-impressive Gwalia Hotel, situated at the entrance to Rock Park, (now the Radnorshire offices of Powys County Council)

A NEW FASHION FOR SPAS

As well as ingesting the waters, a wide range of alternative procedures were on offer, including hydro-electric sulphur baths, carbonic acid baths, cold showers and douches, and scary-sounding pseudo-scientific treatments involving Leucodescent Rays, Galvanic and Faradic Current Cataphoresis, D'Arsonval High Frequency installations and use of the Nagelschmidt Sinusoidal Current apparatus!

BORDERLANDS

The First World War signalled the end of the popularity of Llandrindod Wells and of the other Welsh spa towns of Llangammach, Builth and Llanwrtyd.

With lack of investment and increased competition from Europe, as well as advances in medical knowledge and the advent of sea bathing as a new and fashionable cure, the decline of this and other British spa towns was inevitable.

above: Although a complementary health centre still operates out of the Rock Park Pump Room, the sad remains of the main building now supports only alternative medicinal and exercise regimes.

the merriest sick-resort on earth

Cheltenham Spa
Cheltenham, Gloucestershire

Cheltenham, situated on the edge of the Cotswolds, has been welcoming health-seeking visitors for nearly three hundred years, ever since the recognition of its first natural spring. Although legend suggests that the first medicinal waters were 'discovered' here in 1716 when pigeons were seen pecking at salty deposits around a natural spring, it was a Mr Mason, the land's owner, and in particular his son-in-law Captain Henry Skillicorne (a retired privateer) who should be most credited with the development of Cheltenham as a major spa town. They deepened the well in 1738, erected a building over it and constructed a ballroom and billiard hall on the site.

The Captain also laid out his celebrated 'Well Walk', understanding even then the need to combine an exercise regime alongside the beneficial properties of taking their waters.

above: the Well Walk tea rooms, Cheltenham Spa

The medicinal springs here are said to be the only natural, consumable alkaline waters in Great Britain. Rich in sulphates of magnesium and sodium, combined with bicarbonate of soda, their main benefits to health were considered to be their mildly diuretic and laxative antacid properties.

BORDERLANDS

For five weeks in 1788, King George III, accompanied by his queen and royal princesses, set up court in Cheltenham to take the 'water cure'. And the success of the town as a fashionable spa destination was sealed when early in the nineteenth century, the Duke of Wellington sought and, it seems, found relief here for a liver disorder.

Following these celebrity endorsements, scores more springs were 'discovered' and other pump rooms built, as well as the town's magnificent Regency terraces, squares and ornamental fountains, all of which continued to attract the leading aristocratic figures of the period.

A NEW FASHION FOR SPAS

The Montpellier Spa was developed by Henry Thompson after springs were found on his land in 1801. His spa buildings of 1817 were supplemented by the distinctive Rotunda, designed by John Buonarotti Papworth in 1825. And the Pittville Pump Room – developed by Joseph Pitt in an attempt to rival Cheltenham and set in a beautifully-laid-out park to the north of the town – was completed in 1830.

The waters can still be taken today.

opposite above: the Rotunda Montpellier (once a pump and ballroom, now a Lloyds TSB bank), Cheltenham Spa
(OS Explorer Map No.179: SO 945 218)
opposite below: Neptune Fountain, Cheltenham Spa
(OS Explorer Map No.179: SO 948 225)

right: Pittville Pump Room, Cheltenham
(OS Explorer Map No.179: SO 955 237)

BORDERLANDS

chinese-gothic!

Tenbury Wells

Malvern Hills, Worcestershire
OS Explorer Map No.203: SO 595 679

Tenbury Wells lies on the south bank of the River Teme, which marks the border between Shropshire and Worcestershire. First known as Temettebury, then Tenbury, the 'Wells' was added after the 'discovery' of mineral springs here in the 1840s.

Unquestionably, the most unusual well construction in the country, the Tenbury Wells Victorian Pump Rooms were built in 1862 on the instigation of the Tenbury Improvement Company and designed by James Cranston of Birmingham based upon his existing prefabricated greenhouse designs.

The distinctive structure – often described as 'Chinese-Gothic' in style – was intended to place Tenbury alongside other spa towns like Malvern, Llandrindod, Cheltenham, Leamington and the rest as a leading tourist destination.

Sadly, however, this aim was not fulfilled and the building eventually fell into dereliction.

BORDERLANDS

Tenbury Wells
Pump Rooms

Reopened in 2001, following a major restoration, the Pump Rooms have found new uses as community hall, Register Office and office of the Tenbury Town Clerk.

Tenbury and District Museum Society has recently returned its impressive drinking fountain to the site, together with a cast iron bath from the male bathroom with its unusual feature of four large brass taps – two of which were for mineral water – along with some other interpretative elements to give a stronger impression of the workings of the site.

above left and right:
the Tenbury Pump House bath room:
Note the unusual four-tap bath
(supplying mineral hot and cold and
plain hot and cold water).
above middle: The well at Tenbury is
to be found under glass at the base
of the iconic Pump Rooms tower

opposite the newly-restored
Tenbury Wells fountain

207

the metropolis of hydrotherapy
the wells of the Malvern Hills

I can cure the itchy-pitchy,
Palsy and the gout;
Pains within and pains without,
A broken limb of every sort;
I cured Old Mother Roundabout

from a popular nineteenth century spa song

More than one hundred and thirty springs, spouts, fountains and holy wells have been recorded within the Malvern Hills area on the Herefordshire / Worcestershire border. A circular tour around the foothills takes in most of the main sites in what must surely be the most congested area for well-seekers in the whole of Britain.

The geology here means that the waters are prized for their purity, containing very few minerals (so valued at well sites elsewhere), and with few traces of bacteria or suspended matter:

The Malvern water is famous for containing just nothing at all!

Dr John Wall, on Malvern's Holywell, from his *Experiments and Observations on the Malvern Waters*, 1757

In 1828, William Addison, the physician to the Duchess of Kent (the mother of Queen Victoria) recommended Malvern's "pure and invigorating air, the excellence of its water, and the romantic beauty of its scenery". As a result of these and other recommendations – as well as a number of famous cures – the village of Malvern had become a bustling town by the mid nineteenth century, with its many large hotels and water cure establishments to satisfy all of the needs of the medical tourist:

I have been at Malvern about twelve days, where, with difficulty, I have got a lodging, the place is so full, nor do I wonder at it, there being some instances of very extraordinary cures.

Benjamin Stillingfleet, in a letter to a Mrs Montague, 18 July 1759

Charles Darwin was one of the long list of famous visitors to the Malvern springs, hoping in his case to find a cure for his young daughter. Ironically, he was followed here by the principal opponent of his theory of evolution, Samuel Wilberforce. Others included Florence Nightingale, the founder of modern nursing; the Scottish philospher and essayist Thomas Carlyle; Queen Adelaide of Saxe-Meiningen, the consort of William IV; the Pre-Raphaelite painter Edward Burne-Jones; the poetic Lords Byron and Tennyson; and even the seven year-old US President-to-be, Franklin D Roosevelt. Elizabeth I is said to have drunk Malvern water, and Queen Victoria refused to travel anywhere without it.

And today, Malvern water is what the present queen insists on taking with her on her many travels abroad.

Trips to these water sources, however, were not only made by the rich and the royal; they were from time immemorial, for most of the Malvern Hills' residents, an essential daily routine until the relatively-recent introduction of a pumped domestic mains supply.

above: the Evendine Spring, Malvern Hills
(OS Explorer Map No.190: SO 766 410)

opposite: entrance to the Clock Tower Well,
West Malvern

BORDERLANDS

Walm's Well

Tippin`s Rough, News Wood, south Malvern Hills, near Ledbury, Herefordshire
OS Explorer Map No.190: SO 760 393

Probably the oldest though seemingly one of the least-loved of the Malvern Wells (it could easily have found itself in the next chapter on sadly-neglected sites), Walms is thought by some to have been named after an early Christian missionary:

In Colwall we have Walm`s Well, which yet is much resorted to by the rustics, on account of, what they regard as its admirable curative properties … The Silurian Christian Missionaries Moorall and Walm stood by what we now call Burstner`s Cross and Rye Cross, endeavouring to allure the Celts from the rites and superstitions of their Druid faith.

Surely we may picture woad-dyed Britons trooping from the British Camp to see little children baptised in the Gullet stream, or in the sparkling wells on the slope of the hill.

James McKay, published in
The Malvern Advertiser, 1875

An alternative, and simpler, explanation for the well's name – though much less evocative than that offered by the local journalist – is a corruption of `wielm', the Old English word for spring. Either way, this has been a popular destination for the collection of water, the baptising of converts, and the curing of skin diseases – particularly for those suffering from scurvy and leprosy – for very many centuries.

Sadly, Walm's Well – which once boasted a wooden changing cabin and a stone-clad emersion pool – had fallen into disuse by the mid nineteenth century, although the poet John Masefield (1878-1967) is said to have often visited the site to enjoy its water which he claimed cured "weary eyes and rheumatism" … as well as "broken hearts"! Today, this once-loved spring is encased in concrete and secured by an ugly aluminium door, all enclosed within a rusting padlocked fence.

left above and middle:
Walm's Well and reservoir
left below: the substantial covered reservoir beside Walm's Well

opposite: St Ann's Well,
above Great Malvern

A NEW FASHION FOR SPAS

St Ann's Well and the Old Moses Spout

above Great Malvern, Worcestershire
OS Explorer Map No.190: SO 772 458

Out of thy famous Hille
There daily springeth
A water, passing still,
That always bringeth
Great comfort to alle them
That are diseased men
And makes them well again
So Prayse the Lord!

Rev Edmund Rea, who became Vicar of Great Malvern in 1612, celebrating the curative properties of St Ann's Well

This beautifully-located well on the slopes of the Malvern Hills directly above Great Malvern is probably the most visited of all of the Malvern sacred spring sites. Named today for St Ann, the maternal grandmother of Jesus, legend has it that St Werstan – the Saxon monk and martyr-to-be – found sanctuary here after the destruction of his monastery at Deerhurst in Gloucestershire in the mid eleventh century. Perhaps the similarity of the sounds of the words 'St Ann' and 'Werstan' is no coincidence and the former was a re-dedication – common in well lore – based upon the latter.

Some, however, have suggested a much earlier authority, that of the Celtic water goddess, Anu, or even a dedication to the spirit of the sun (the Welsh word for fire is 'tan').

Whatever its origin or etymology, the waters here were recognised for their purity from earliest times, offering cures for "many maladies suffered by mediaeval folk" (CF Burrow, *A little city set on the hill: the story of Malvern*, 1948). As well as 'taking the waters', free hot and cold baths were available here, and Great Malvern and St Ann's began to eclipse the facilities at their longer established neighbour, Malvern Springs.

The building which currently houses the waters was erected in 1813, and its octagonal extension – now a café – in 1860. In 1892, a finely-carved Sicilian marble water spout in the form of a dolphin's head and a shell-shaped basin was donated by Lady Emily Foley, the site's owner. The plaque over the basin reads:

Drink of this crystal fountain
And praise the loving Lord
Who from the rocky mountain
This living stream out-poured
Fit emblem of the Holy fount
That flows from God's eternal mount.

Rev W Blake Atkinson, rector of Bradley near Redditch

From the early years of the nineteenth century, teams of donkeys were available for hire to carry well-healed visitors up the steep and winding slope from their expensive hotels in Great Malvern and elsewhere to St Ann's, one of the highest of the Malvern springs. And, for nearly fifty years between 1880 and 1930, once at the top, if you were lucky, you might be entertained by blind euphonium and dulcitone player, George Pullen.

It was widely reported that one of the Malvern Hills donkeys called Moses carried the eleven year-old Princess Victoria up the zig-zag path to St Ann's in 1830 … wrong, unfortunately, on three counts.

Firstly, it was the Dowager Queen Adelaide who was the passenger and who re-christened the creature 'Royal Moses' for his troubles; the year in question was 1843 not 1830; and, although the Princess was in Malvern, accompanied by her mother, the Duchess of Kent in 1830, their status precluded them from riding on local beasts, bringing with them their own donkeys and mules for the duration of their stay.

Despite all of this – and not wanting the facts get in the way of a good story – the legend of Moses and the Princess still persists. On 9 December 2005, it was re-told at the well-blessing – and re-naming as 'Old Moses Spout' – of the trough next to the well house at St Ann's from which the exhausted animals drank on arriving with their burdens.

The tale, however, has a sad ending, the popularity of the animal as a mount causing his early demise just a few short years later, "the poor beast … being ridden to death" after the royal's assessment of Moses as "the premiership among Malvern asses"!

above: the Old Moses Spout, situated next to St Ann's Well, Malvern Hills

left: the basin at St Ann's Well, above Great Malvern

Holy Well

Holy Well Road, Malvern Wells, Worcestershire
OS Explorer Map No.190: SO 770 423

The 'holy' in Holy Well's name is thought to stem from its association with St Oswald (most likely the tenth century Bishop of Worcester, not the seventh century King of Northumberland encountered in Chapter Four: *Holy Wells in the Age of the Warrior Princes*). It was he who is said to have revealed the curative properties of the site to a local hermit. Traditionally, the spring was 'dressed' on the saint's day by people who had received a miracle cure from its waters.

Holy Well's reputation for healing was being widely reported as far back as the mid sixteenth century. It had, it seems, a range of remedies for ailments as diverse as eye disorders, ulcers, cancers, skin diseases, glandular obstructions and kidney complaints, for which the patient was instructed to drink as well as bath within and, sometimes even, wrap oneself in sheets soaked in its waters.

Holy Well is claimed to be the place where Malvern spring water was bottled on a commercial basis for the very first time, from 1622 onwards. Indeed, the site is probably the oldest bottling plant in the world.

From 1850, the water was extracted and distributed on an industrial scale by Schweppes, which, as the official caterers to the 1851 Great Exhibition, introduced 'Malvern Soda' to the world.

opposite: the author's mother

above: entrance to the Holy Well, Malvern Wells

right: well dressing at Holy Well, April 2010 (a tradition that was resurrected in the MalvernHills in 1993)

at the Holy Well dressing

BORDERLANDS

Today, the tradition is continued on the site by a small family-owned business, the Holywell Water Company, which won back the rights to use the name from Coca-Cola (who now own Schweppes) after they closed their plant in the area in 2010 and, initially, refused permission for any other firm to use the brand name:

It's in a glass bottle and we believe it should be a premium product. Coca-Cola put Malvern in a plastic bottle and sold it in vending machines. It was so sad.

Rhys Humm, current Holywell Water Company director

above and right:
the Holy Well bottling plant today

A NEW FASHION FOR SPAS

Earl Beauchamp's Fountain

Cowleigh Road, Malvern Hills, Worcestershire
OS Explorer Map No.190:
SO 766 475

Formerly known as the Cowleigh Spout for its location on the Cowleigh Road, the daily output here is in excess of ten thousand gallons.

The 'Fountain' was presented to the people of Cowleigh in 1905 by William Earl Beauchamp, who was to be immortalised later as Lord Marchmain in Evelyn Waugh's *Brideshead Revisited*.

It is said to continue to flow even in the most severe of droughts, often in the past making it a life-saving feature of an area where springs regularly run dry during extended periods of little or no rain.

below: the Cope family at Earl Beauchamp's Fountain, well-dressed on a Maytime theme, April 2010
right: Earl Beauchamp's Fountain

A NEW FASHION FOR SPAS

opposite: **Evendine Spring**, Brand Green, Malvern Hills, Worcestershire, considered by many to offer the finest water in the Hills

above: The Evendine is a popular water fill-up point.
below: well-dressing on the theme of Florence Nightingale on the centenary of her death, Evendine Spring, April 2010

right and opposite middle: The so-called Hospital Fountain (OS Explorer Map No. 190: SO 781 474) – in the small Heritage Hall on the first floor of the Malvern Community Hospital on Worcester Road in Malvern Link - was originally located at the Cottage Hospital in Landsdowne Crescent. It was moved to its present position in 2011.

A NEW FASHION FOR SPAS

Malvern Community Hospital

above: The Hospital Fountain won a St Werstan Award in August 2011.

BORDERLANDS

Hay Slad Spout
West Malvern Road, Malvern Hills
OS Explorer Map No.190: SO 766 448

Possibly the most popular place to fill up with free Malvern spring water, Hay Slad's twin spouts and basin is, like many others on the Malvern Hills, fed by springs in the hills above, and channelled to the roadside for more convenient collection.

The 'slad' in Hay Slad probably comes from the Norwegian word for valley, or perhaps, more appropriately, 'slade', Old English for an area of low boggy land which the site would certainly have originally been, sat below the springs before the spout was built.

above: always busy water collection at the ever-constant Hay Slad Spout
left: the Hay Slad Spout during the Malvern Hills Well Dressing Festival, April 2010

opposite: **Westminster Bank Spout**
(OS Explorer Map No.190: SO 765 462)

left above: Behind this spout on Westminster Bank sit a number of water tanks from which the main supplies were pumped to much of West Malvern during the nineteenth and left: The Westminster Bank Spout provides a tiered series of troughs to satisfy the thirsts of passing humans, and of creatures great and small.

The Clock Tower Well and Water Tank

West Malvern Road, North Malvern, Worcestershire
OS Explorer Map No.190: SO 770 471

Such was the popularity of this area that the number of residents of Great Malvern almost doubled in the decade between 1851 and 1861, while the fragile – exacerbated by the hot summers and years of low rainfall – meant that no increase in the delivery of water was possible without a substantial investment.

Following a public debate in 1871, the hillside above the already-existing 43,500 gallon-capacity Malvern Tower water tank was chosen as the site for a new one million gallon chamber to satisfy the rapidly-growing demand.

Despite many early mishaps, work on the new tank – designed by the somewhat-under-qualified town surveyor – began at the end of 1872 and was eventually completed some five years later.

the Clock Tower

BORDERLANDS

below: steps up to, and site of the 'new' one million gallon Water Tank, above the Clock Tower

opposite: the Clock Tower spout and basin

On a cold February afternoon in 1877, it was ceremonially opened at a grand event attended by some fifteen hundred local people and visitors:

The commanding escarpment of the hill ... was gay with bannerets and streamers, with the sound of the harp and fiddle, the trumpet and the drum, the applause of men, and the merry voices of women and little ones. Immediately below the new reservoir there is a huge cairn of debris, and on an inclined plane immediately above this a steam lift has been in use ... 'draped in pink and carpeted for the use of the ladies'... so as to safely and comfortably transport about a dozen ladies at a time. From two o'clock until five it was incessantly in requisition raising bevies of belles from the road to the mouth of the reservoir in the rocks, over a hundred feet above ...

local newspaper report on the 1877 Clock Tower Tank opening ceremony

An extra storey and a new clock with four gas-lit faces were added to the Tower in 1901 to celebrate the coronation of Edward VII, with further restorations taking place in 2006 and 2007. The Clock Tower was officially re-opened on Sunday 3 May 2009, with the water flow fully-restored to the site in a ceremony which gave thanks for the constancy of the gifts of water here, and made moving reference to large areas of the world much less blessed.

a renewed curiosity

The spa age was a unique episode in social history, fascinating for its contrasts between artificial languishings and cultivated fragility and those imposed mortifications of the flesh, in health's name, that today would try an athlete in perfect physical condition …

Muriel Searle
from her *Spa and Watering Places*, 1977

In time, the treatments on offer at our spa towns were to be replaced by a new kind of hydrotherapy, available now at seaside resorts, alongside the added benefits of sunlight, aromatic pines and bracing sea air.

In addition, local authorities were beginning to provide more easily accessible and cheaper alternatives to the spas in their municipal baths and swimming pools.

And the advances in medical knowledge that culminated in the creation of the Nation Health Service in 1948 offered effective treatments for all the ailments that the spas claimed to relieve, resulting in the decline and closure of most of these once-thriving establishments.

A NEW FASHION FOR SPAS

In the late twentieth century, however, a growing recognition of the damage we are doing to our planet, alongside an uneasiness with our increased reliance on prescription drugs, sparked a renewed curiosity in and search for alternative remedies, far distanced from the reach of the global pharmaceutical industry.

Today, in Britain and throughout the world, a new interest in sacred springs, holy wells and curative waters is being witnessed, as new spa centres are being developed, often along the lines of those with which the Romans would have been familiar, but without, perhaps, the fellowship or good offices of an all-powerful deity.

opposite: These new iron gates for the Clock Tower were designed by Rose Garrard and constructed by Andrew Findlay of Eastnor Forge for the re-opening event in May 2009.

above: the author's daughter at the well-dressed Malvhina Fountain, Great Malvern, April 2010

Enigma Fountain

Belle Vue Island, Great Malvern,
Worcestershire
OS Explorer Map No.190: SO 775 460

A fine work by the sculptor Rose Garrard – located within the Belle Vue Terrace Island in the centre of Great Malvern – Enigma is dedicated to the Worcestershire composer Edward Elgar who is buried next to his wife at St Wulstan's Church in Little Malvern, and drew much of his inspiration from the beauty of the area.

Garrard's Enigma combines both water and music, two major elements in the area's cultural history.

Funded by the Malvern Hills District Council and public subscription, with support from Severn Trent Water, West Midlands Arts and local businesses, the Enigma Fountain was unveiled on 26 May 2000 by the Duke of York.

opposite: Enigma Fountain, Great Malvern

above: Malvhina Fountain, Great Malvern

BORDERLANDS

Malvhina Fountain

Belle Vue Island, Great Malvern,
Worcestershire
OS Explorer Map No.190: SO 775 459

Following a two-month artist's residency in 1997, Rose Garrard was also commissioned by Malvern Hills District Council to create this drinking spout (with sponsorship from West Midlands Arts and the Elmley Foundation). Entitled Malvhina, the work is based upon three themes suggested by local people. These are the artist's words:

"Its form reflects ancient Celtic standing stones with spiral markings, medieval religious statuary and Victorian Pre-Raphaelite imagery, suggesting three of the most magnificent periods in Malvern's history

The Malvern spring water flows from a bronze disc where three circles interlink symbolising the sacred triple of the Celts, the Christian Holy Trinity and the three springs above the Town, Happy Valley, Rushey Valley and Ivy Scar Rock, which combine here. The sculpture is named Malvhina after a Celtic Princess which some Victorian historians romantically connected with Malvern itself.

Malvhina was unveiled on 4 September 1998.

Malvhina Fountain, Great Malvern

ON THE BORDERLANDS OF DECAY
holy wells into the twenty-first century

Hollis Brown
He lived on the outside of town
Hollis Brown
He lived on the outside of town
With his wife and five children
And his cabin brokin' down.

Your grass is turning black
There's no water in your well
Your grass is turning black
There's no water in your well

You spent your last lone dollar
On seven shotgun shells.

Bob Dylan
from *Ballad of Hollis Brown*

opposite: broken bath tub,
Llangammarch Wells, Breconshire / Powys

above: the Old Bridge Well, Llanfyllin,
Mongomeryshire / Powys

BORDERLANDS

The springs, wells and spas of the Borderlands can still today provide us with a cornucopia of colourful sights, moving stories and inspiring experiences. But the picture is not all rosy.

While places like St Winefride's in Holywell and the Virtuous Well at Trellech continue to thrive as centres for contemplation, communion and healing, and some others like St Peter's in Peterchurch have found a contemporary use for their ancient waters while retaining their connections with a rich past, many of our once-treasured sacred sites have been or are in the process of being destroyed. While special places like Ffynnon Elian in Denbighshire, once neglected are today being lovingly restored, and, in a very few cases, new wells are even being added to our Borderland inventory – most successfully in the Malvern Hills area – very many more are being lost … to farming, to drainage, to road-widening schemes, to new housing or simple indifference and neglect.

Sacred and holy sites once seen as an essential part of the ritual of our daily lives are now regularly buried beneath piles of rubble, built over by a new bridge or housing development without a second thought, or ploughed up by farmers frustrated with having to swerve their tractors around another pile of old stones. This, regrettably, is an important chapter in our story of holy wells in the twenty-first century.

the 'sometime' mansion

Sutton Wells Hillfort Well

Sutton Wells Iron Age Fort
Sutton St Michael, near Marden, Herefordshire
OS Landranger Map no.149:
SO 525 464

notable ruines of some auncyent and great building, sumtyme the mansion of King Offa, at such time Kenchestre stood, or els Herford was a begynning.

John Leland (c.1503-1552), English poet and antiquarian, writing about Sutton Walls Iron Age Fort in the early sixteenth century

Celebrated as the Palace of King Offa, this is where Ethelbert is said to have been murdered by the king while on his way to marry the Mercian leader's daughter (a story we explored in the *Age of the Saints* Chapter, p.99).

This is certainly a place which has been bathed in more than its fair share of blood. Attacked almost from its earliest days, most forcefully by the Romans, this was the site of massacres and mass burials. In later years, the place was regularly quarried for its stione, until its most recent invaders arrived, toxic chemicals from the twentieth century.

The well here today, which would have serviced all of its struggling inhabitants through history, has been crudely-capped to quench contemporary thirsts for water if not for beauty.

left: Sutton Walls hillfort
above: Sutton Walls capped well

HOLY WELLS INTO THE TWENTY-FIRST CENTURY

While I am no great fan of the spiritless (though award-winning) renovation of St Myllin's Well in Llanfyllin, Mongomeryshire / Powys (OS Landranger Map No.125: SJ 138 196), worse still awaits at the second well site in the village, the Old Bridge Well (OS Landranger Map No.125: SJ 142 195) which is currently used by local people as a convenient receptacle for rubbish bags.

Whistlebitch Well

near Utkinton, Cheshire
OS Explorer Map No.267: SJ 549 670

Although its life was a short one, the importance of Whistlebitch in the annals of well lore should not be forgotten. From a sleepy backwater of a village to a thriving nationally-important well destination welcoming at its height more than 2,000 cure seekers a day, Utkinton's transformation was quite-literally overnight, following the London publication in the year 1600 of a pamphlet by one GW, entitled *Newes out of Cheshire concerning the New found Well*.

The article told of one John Greeneway of Utkinton "an honest subsantiall countriman of good credit and well reputed", who was "troubled with the Fittes" being advised by his doctor to find a "prettie purling fountaine", where "by drinking, washing and accomplishing what he was commaunded, in verie shorte time hee was of his Ague throughly cured".

Going on to list many other miraculous cures at Utkinton – including that of a Robert Bradley, "who … was led hither blind, hath here recouered sight, and … is gone home without leading" – the author celebrated the waters for their cures "not onely against Agues… but also against all manner of coldes, stoppings, grypings, gnawings, collicks, aches, ruptures & inward infirmities, and no lesse soueraigne against sores and outward anguishes, wounds, swellings, vlcers, festers, impostumes and hurts of the seuerall ioynts and members; besides that, it hath done no small number of straunge cures, against sorenes of eyes and eares, blindnesse, deafenesse, lamenesse, stifnesse of sinnewes, numbnesse, weakenesse and feeblenesse, all which I am able to auerre and proue, by undeniable demonstration from the seuerall effects of infinite numbers of people, that haue giuen witnesse thereof in these three or foure moneths now last past".

Such a comprehensive list of cures was bound to do the trick and thousands flocked to Whistlebitch Well and Utkinton, which quickly developed all of the necessary facilities to support the new demand with shops and guesthouses, dams to trap the waters as they fell down the hillside, and fountains, lakes and pools in which its visitors could drink and bathe.

Initially tolerated by the crown, on whose lands the well sat, Whistlebitch was later perceived to be a threat to the Queen's deer forest and the phenomenally successful site was forced to close within three short years of the publication of the London pamphlet, and Utkinton fell back into obscurity.

Today, with a strong imagination and a pair of water-tight boots, it is still possible to retrace the path up the valley from the remains of the Whistlebitch pump house, passing what little survives of the dams and the tanks, to the site of the old well, and to hear, perhaps, a few faint echoes of the three chaotic years of prayers granted and refused here.

HOLY WELLS INTO THE TWENTY-FIRST CENTURY

above: Whistlebitch Well, Utkinton, Cheshire

opposite: what remains of the holding tank and pump house, Whistlebitch Well

There are a number of old well sites in the area of land now known as Grosvenor Park on the north bank of the river Dee in Chester.

left and above: The so-called
Billy Hobby's Well
(OS Explorer Map No.266: SJ 413 662) – situated in what was known once as Billy Obbies' Field – was said to have had magical properties. Young women would stand with their right legs in the waters here to wish for husbands!

HOLY WELLS INTO THE TWENTY-FIRST CENTURY

below: the unloved shell of the now-dry Jacob's Well drinking fountain in Grosvenor Park, Chester (OS Explorer Map No.266: SJ 412 663)

The Wells

Cleobury Mortimer, Shropshire
OS Explorer Map No.203: SO 675 758

The Cleobury Mortimer Wells – fed from a local spring in the churchyard – were for centuries the main public water supply of this important Shropshire market town, although the wisdom of situating the Wells on land below the graveyard was regularly questioned, especially in Victorian times when fears of contagion from waterbourne diseases such as typhus and cholera were rife. In 1883, burials within forty-two yards of the town Wells were prohibited, and eventually, in 1895, the whole churchyard was closed down.

right: The Wells, Cleobury Mortimer

In 2010, the flow to the Wells inexplicably ceased, and the tank remains dry to this day, a sad end for what was once an important civic amenity, albeit one which provided a regular headache for its citizens.

241

BORDERLANDS

Llanwrtyd Wells

Radnorshire / Powys
OS Landranger Map No.147:
SN 872 470

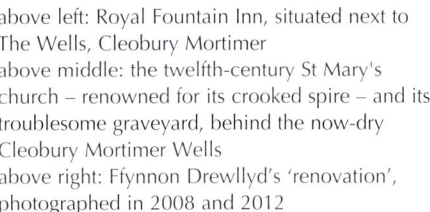

above left: Royal Fountain Inn, situated next to The Wells, Cleobury Mortimer
above middle: the twelfth-century St Mary's church – renowned for its crooked spire – and its troublesome graveyard, behind the now-dry Cleobury Mortimer Wells
above right: Ffynnon Drewllyd's 'renovation', photographed in 2008 and 2012

I have been watching the developments of this once-important spa town site for many years. Based around the so-called Ffynnon Ddrewllyd (or 'stinking' spring), whose hydrogen sulphide healing properties were 'discovered' in 1732 by the Rev Theophilus Evans, Llanwrtyd Wells grew into a major Welsh spa town on the River Irfon.

Old Pump-house, Llanwrtyd Wells

The door is open. I shall not be intruding,
going in to sit on the bench by the wall,
to breathe the stuffy dankness streaked with sulphur,
and stare through broken panes over the shaggy grounds.
This sociable place has died through lack of visiting.
A pungent drip, still slowly forced from the spring's heart,
has grown a fungus-garden in the great mirrored basin.
Some chairs lie on the sheep-fouled floor,
some lurch, still conversationally grouped,
against the counter over which was handed
health by the tumblerful when crowds came here,
laughing and garrulous, to take the waters;
pulling faces over the taste of their cure,
and bragging of the glasses they had drunk
like boys about their beer. They came streaming
six times a day from the bursting village
to jostle and gossip round the sulphur-bar.
Sheep-farmers, knitting wives, holiday miners
from the black valleys, jam-packed the houses,
ate meals in shifts, and sat outside singing hymns
on the suddenly hushed street of evening;
or went back in warm dusk to the well-house
to hear the Builth harper play under summer trees
and watch youngsters dance.
The plucked notes, never wholly gay, and laughing voices
spiralled up through the trees, up the long valley;
and lost themselves among the hills
over the sealed frontier of the past.

Ruth Bidgood

BORDERLANDS

As we have seen elswhere, the development of a spa facility meant prosperity for the area concerned, with the building of fine new hotels, inns, shops and treatment centres to cater for the vistor's every need.

With the demise of the movement in Britain, however, the town – claimed to be the smallest in Britain – had to find new reasons to survive once the spa tourists had departed for good. This it did with the invention of mountain bike trails, beer festivals and, most imaginatively, the annual Man versus Horse Marathons and the World Bog Snorkling Championships.

The same cannot be said, it seems, of the renovations taking place at the spa site. For years the buildings sat derelict. Now they are being converted into homes and the domed well housing has been demolished, a new conservatory-style extension erected in its place surrounding the mosaic-decorated well basin which at its height could deliver up to 4,500 gallons of sulphur-rich water a day.

above: members of the Victorian Society at the magnificent marble well basin, Ffynnon Drewllyd, on a wells tour led by the author, June 2012
below: Ffynnon Drewllyd's mosaic-decorated well basin

HOLY WELLS INTO THE TWENTY-FIRST CENTURY

left: **Llangammarch Wells**, near Builth Wells, Breconshire / Powys (OS Landranger Map No.147: SN 945 476) was the smallest of the four spa villages of mid-Wales (alongside Llandrindod, Builth and Llanwrtyd Wells).
Now lying in ruins on the banks of the river Irfon, the Llangammarch well house once offered the questionable benefits of barium-rich waters.

BORDERLANDS

Ffynnon Ddyfnog

Llanrhaeadr-yng-Nghinmeirch, Denbighshire
OS Landranger Map No 116:
SJ 081 633

there is nothing we suffer to get so near us as the tokens of the remote.

Henry James (1843-1916)
Cathedrals and Castles, 1905

Ffynnon Ddyfnog in Llanrhaeadr-yng-Nghinmeirch, Denbighshire was featured as the front cover image and as a major chapter in my first book on holy wells, *Holy Wells, Wales: a photographic journey* (Seren, ISBN 978-1-85411-485-3, 2008).

Approached through a wooded dell some two hundred metres to the west of the famous church with its fine sixteenth century Jesse window, pilgrims have sought out this holy space for many centuries.

Sadly, today, however, its springs are threatened by a landslip and, most worryingly, the fine arched bridge under which the waters flow to the valley below from its large bathing pool – in whose freezing waters the ascetic St Dyfnog would have stood to do his penance – is in serious danger of collapse.

opposite:
the author and anthologist
Dewi Roberts
at Ffynnon Ddyfnog

BORDERLANDS

right: Ffynnon Ddyfnog

opposite:
Venta Silurum / Caerwent,
Monmouthshire

But, in reality, the place I visited for my first book is not so different from what I saw during my latest visit, some six years later for this one, especially if you listen to the accounts of the elaborate site in its heyday when it was furnished with a roof, and when the pool had a marble floor; when there were rooms provided for pilgrims in which to change their clothes; and when images of saints filled the niches in its walls.

A complex combination of this developing tradition since the first discovery of the waters' healing properties, followed by Protestant attacks on Catholic holy water practices during the Reformation, the slow but powerful pulse of nature – alongside simple human neglect – has created the sight I saw then and what you will see, today.

But I wonder if it is the original experience we ever really crave, anyway.

The tiny valley packed with the sick and the lame – and with those self-appointed to serve them – would have been a very different place from that which greets us now, open as it is to the trees and the sky … and to the imagination.

The very good news here is that a steering group made up of local people working alongside a firm of architects experienced in the renovation of historical sites has been established, plans drawn up and a fundraising campaign launched to address the urgent conservation issues of the bridge's collapse.

In addition, they will be investigating the longer-term environmental, community and spiritual needs of this old site for our new times.

It's certain that further deterioration needs to be halted here, but perhaps, as Henry James suggested, our search is now for the "tokens of the remote" rather than for the "remote" itself.

St Winifred's in Holywell when packed with bathers on a hot weekend, or even the banks of the Ganges at Varanasi at the height of its festivities both felt to me more like Barry Island on a Bank Holiday Monday than the sanctified sites I had conjured.

What remains of our once-elaborate well sites, and what we seem to value most, are mere glimpses of a distant and silenced past at which we may not have felt as comfortable in their heydays as we now do alongside their remnants.

Like both our real and our imagined journeys to ancient places – their columns once upright and brightly-painted, their temples thronged with worshipers – I, for one, seem happiest to sit alone amongst the stark and tumbled ruins, now washed clean of too much artifice by the rain and bleached white by the sun.

* HUNTING THE PLUCK OF WATER
a few last words ...

opposite: St Winefride's Well, Holywell, Flintshire

above: Ffynnon Fair, Trefnant, Denbighshire

Life is only comprehensible through a thousand local Gods. And not just the old dead ones with names like Zeus – no, but living geniuses of Place and Person!

the character Dysart speaking in
Peter Shaffer's play, *Equus*, 1973

As a cult it has forsaken the busy haunts of men, but lingers still in quiet places ... Superstitions die hard. The epitaph of this one has still to be written. Those who are waiting for its last breath need not be surprised if they have to wait yet a while.

James Murray Mackinlay
Folklore of Scottish Lochs and Springs, 1893

This has been a long walk through history and through belief, studded on both sides of our broad Borderland path with sacred springs and revered trees; with saints and their holy wells; with bath houses, spouts and healing spas; with rivers, streams and their crossings; and with carved stones, ancient mounds and forts, towering castles, chapels, churches and cathedrals, left in ruins or restored, all of which tell parts of the story of where we have been and what we have mostly forgotten.

* Seamus Heaney, from *The Diviner*, (*Death of a Naturalist*, 1966)

BORDERLANDS

Dr Henry Jacob, speaking about the contested, some-would-say mythical life of St Werstan, the patron saint of Malvern Springs and Wells in his 1919 lecture entitled *Malvern Past and Present*, made the plea that "this beautiful legend would not be summarily consigned to the limbo of discredited fable". And, in 2005, the St Werstan Award Scheme was established to recognise those who had contributed to the protection and enhancement of the Malvern Hills well sites. So even if the saint didn't exist, he does now!

The land and what our hands, and our imaginations, have added to it – and in particular, in the case of this volume, the ways in which we have tried to understand the various gifts of clean refreshing waters gushing unbidden from the earth – all offer a rich library of alternative explanations for the unexplainable.

The physical remains, recorded histories, and legends all connect us, albeit loosely, to the minds and the emotions of our ancestors, with all of their gullibility, lack of logic and profound wisdom. And, even though the stories that have been handed down are often dependant upon which version has dominated through time, each still contains a tiny particle of this wider, ultimately-unattainable, and often contradictory truth: Was Ffynnon Elian in Denbighshire a cursing well as the local Methodist church would have had you believe, or a site at which to seek a measure of justice for an oppressed nation? How much of the stories of the saints Ethelbert, Kenelm, Dubricius, Winifride, Chad and Milburga actually happened? Could Owain Glyndŵr really control the weather, and how effective a cure-all was Llandrindod Wells' Nagelschmidt Sinusoidal Current apparatus?

Many of these ancient tales and more-recent claims, of course, seem to be bordering on the ridiculous now that their originators' metaphysics has become our physics, their poetry our science … but some of the poetry remains. Despite the sad evidence of the destruction and neglect of many holy sites, there are still some enchanted places to visit and, on very special occasions, at which to be inspired at the discovery of a totally-abandoned but still intact well with its watery prize. And it's at these moments that this potential dialogue with those powerful and compelling Borderland places between our everyday reality and another more strange conviction becomes so enriching and so essential.

It is then that a contact is offered with people and beliefs long neglected, but continuing to offer some albeit-vague answers to questions we haven't yet been able to perfectly formulate, questions which lead us perhaps, in the words of Peter J Conradi a little way towards "the recovery of the sacred". (*At the Bright Hem of God: Radnorshire Pastoral*, 2009)

I want to end with a final quote which I think is worthy of reprinting, despite its length and its age.

It encapsulates for me the reasons for re-visiting sacred springs and holy wells in our busy and conflicted world, and reinforces the argument to protect these ancient places which keep us connected to the mysteries of a reverberating past:

left: Trefriw Spa, Conwy

A FEW LAST WORDS

The lover of romance and sentiment, and even the least susceptible to the charms of nature, will never grow weary of the creed which tells him that the sparkling waters are the haunt of laughing nymphs or listening saints, and that in the glint of streams, or the placidity of deep, cool wells may be detected the reflection of the visage of the attendant sprite. There is something too felicitous in the idea to abandon it willingly; something too alluring in the fancy to submit it to a too rigid analysis of science. A wealth of mediaeval lore has gathered about the revered places where the watersprings bubble, and they preserve the names of many blessed men and women, who, by their good deeds, deserve so delightful a memorial.

For ourselves we are ready to say, let benedictions still be uttered by the water's edge, let the old wells still be decked with mottoes and wreaths, let the villagers still assemble to offer alms or to receive, and even let the crooked pins still be dropped to propitiate a patron saint, or to satisfy a shy maiden's anxiety as to the devotion of her lover. These are the superstitions and observances which are rather to be encouraged than despised, for they link us with generations of the past, and in pleasant, unoffending form draw continuous attention upon those places of balm and reflection which our ancestors not unfittingly deemed consecrated and to which they therefore rendered homage or worship simple and more dignified than a senseless crouching before idols.

Cuming Walters
from *The Church Treasury*, 1898

Index of Sites

Abby Cwmhir 162
Abergavenny Castle 163
Balineae Silures, Castell Colwen 68
Beeston Castle, Tarporley 174
Billy Hobby's Well, Grosvenor Park 240
Bronllys Castle, Talgarth 171
Cheltenham Spa 201
Cleobury Mortimer 24
Depplewell, Moccas 40
Droitwich Spa, Droitwich 189
Earl Beauchamp's Fountain, Malvern Hills 217
Enigma Fountain, Great Malvern 231
Evendine Spring, Malvern Hills 219
Ffynnon Beuno, Gwyddelwern 115
Ffynnon Beuno, Tremeirchion 114
Ffynnon Ddyfnog, Llanrhaeadr-yng-Nghinmeirch 246
Ffynnon Degla, Llandegla 38
Ffynnon Elian, Llanelian 34
Ffynnon Fair, Llanfair Caereinion 82
Ffynnon Fair, Trefnant 84
Ffynnon Gybi, Llangybi 97
Ffynnon Gynhafal, Llangynhafal 122
Glyndyfrdwy Mound 165
Havelock Well, Much Wenlock 47
Hay Slad Spout, Malvern Hills 222
Holy Well, Malvern Wells 215
Holy Well of St Dubricious, Hentland 93
Hospital Fountain, Malvern Link 220
Isca Augusta, Caerleon 60
Jacob's Well, Grosvenor Park 241
Litchfield Cathedral 129
Llandrindod Wells 194
Llangammarch Wells 245
Llanwrtyd Wells 242
Llywelyn ap Gruffydd's Well, Cilmeri 160
Ludlow Castle 176
Noden's Temple, Lydney 63
Malvhina Fountain, Great Malvern 232
Mary's Well, Bodrhyddan Hall 80
Nantwich 192
Northwich 193
Old Bridge Well, Llanfyllin 237
Our Lady Well, Hempstead 79
Prestatyn Roman Bath House 71
Raglan Castle 181
St Ann's Well, Aconbury 43
St Ann's Well, Great Malvern 211
St Anthony's Well, Cinderford 88
St Chad's Well, Chadkirk 127
St Chad's Well, Lichfield 128
St Ethelbert's Well, Castle Green 101
St Ethelbert's Well, Marden 100
St John the Baptist Holy Well, Hope Bagot 29
St Julian's Well, Ludlow 90
St Kenelm's Well, Romsley 134
St Kenelm's Well, Winchcombe 137
St Mary's Well, Pilleth 167
St Milburga's Well, Much Wenlock 122
St Milburga's Well, Stoke St Milburga 121
St Oswald's Well, Holywell 152
St Oswald's Well, Maserfield 151
St Oswald's Well, Winwick 148
St Peter's Well, Peterchurch 33
St Tewdrig's Well, Mathern 146
St Thomas's Holy Well, Llanveynoe 25
St Winefride's Well, Holywell 106
St Winefride's Well, Woolston 110
Stokesay Castle, Craven Arms 178
Strata Florida 154
Sutton Wells Hillfort Well, Sutton St Michael 236
Sycarth Castle 164
Tenbury Wells Pump Rooms 204
The Clock Tower Well, North Malvern 224
The Holy Well, Alderley Edge 24
The Virtuous Well, Trellech 43
The Wishing Well, Alderley Edge 23
The Wizard's Well, Alderley Edge 22
Trefiw Spa, Trefiw 187
Venta Silurum, Caerwent 64
Viroconium Cornoviorum, Wroxeter 53
Walm's Well, Malvern Hills 210
New Weir Water Shrine, Swainshill 72
Wenlock Priory, Much Wenlock 117
Westminster Bank Spout, Malvern Hills 223
Whistlebitch Well, Utkinton 238
Winchombe Abbey 141

Acknowledgements

'Old Pump-house: Llanwrtd Wells' by Ruth Bidgood is taken from her *New & Selected Poems* (Seren, 2004)

'Welsh Landscape' by R.S. Thomas is reproduced by permission of Kunjana Thomas

Selected Further Reading

Gabriel Alington, *Borderlands, a history and romance of the Herefordshire Marches*, 1998
Janet Bord, *Holy Wells in Britain: a guide*, 2008
Augustus Bozzi Granville, *The Spas of England, and Principal Sea-Bathing Places: Midland Spas*, 1841
Edith Brill, *Life and Tradition on the Cotswolds*, 1973
Charlotte Sophie Burne / Georgina F Jackson, *Shropshire Folk-Lore, a sheaf of gleanings*, 1883
Peter J Conradi, *At the Bright Hem of God, Radnorshire Pastoral*, 2009
John Davies, *A History of Wales*, 1993
Andrew and Annelise Fielding, *The Salt Industry*, 2006
Jeremy Harte, *England Holy Wells, a source-book*, 2008
Christina Hole, *Traditions and Customs of Cheshire*, 1937
RC Hope, *The Legendary Lore of the Holy Wells of England*, 1893
Simon James, *Exploring the World of The Celts*, 1993
Rev Francis Kilvert, *Selections from the Diary 1870-79*, 1938-40
Ella Mary Leather, *The Folklore of Herefordshire*, 1912
Kari Maund, *The Welsh Kings: Warriors, Warlocks and Saints*, 2000
Nick Mayhew Smith, *Britain's Holiest Places*, 2011
Prys Morgan (ed.), *History of Wales, 25,000BC - AD 2000*, 2001
Jan Morris, *Wales, Epic Views of a Small Country*, 1984
VE Nash-Williams, *The Roman Frontier in Wales*, 1954
Bruce Osborne and Cora Weaver, *Celebrated Springs of the Malvern Hills*, 2012
Roy Palmer, The *Folklore of Warwickshire*, 1976
Roy Palmer, The *Folklore of Hereford & Worcester*, 1992
Roy Palmer, *Folklore of Gloucestershire*, 1994
Roy Palmer, *The Folklore of (old) Monmouthshire*, 1998
Roy Palmer, *Folklore of Radnorshire*, 2001
Roy Palmer, *Herefordshire Folklore*, 2002
Roy Palmer, The *Folklore of Shropshire*, 2004
J Rattue, *The Living Stream: Holy Wells in Historical Context*, 1995
Graham Roberts, *Around and About Herefordshire and the Southern Welsh Marches*, 2004
Ian D Rotheram, *Roman Baths in Britain*, 2012
Jonathan Sant, *Healing Wells of Herefordshire*, 1994
Jacqueline Simpson, *Folklore of the Welsh Border*, 1976
Lewis Spence, *The Mysteries of Britain: Sacred Rites and Traditions in Ancient Britain*, 1905
Gerry Stewart, *St Kenelm's Way (from Clent to Cotswold)*, 2005
Richard Suggett, *A History of Magic and Witchcraft in Wales*, 2008
N Summerton, *Medicine and Health Care in Roman Britain*, 2007
Ian & Frances Thompson, *The Water of Life: Springs and Wells of Mainland Britain*, 2004
Cuming Walters, *Holy Wells*, 1898
RC Skyring Walters, *The Ancient Wells, Springs and Holy Wells of Gloucestershire*, 1928
Raymond Williams, *Border Country*, 1960
Roger JA Wilson, *A Guide to the Roman Remains in Britain*, 1975
Sarah and John Zaluckyj, *The Celtic Christian Sites of the Central and Southern Marches*, 2006

a simple farm well found in a field at the bottom of Sutton Walls after a frustrating day's well-hunting, one of those surprising unrecorded gifts that well sites sometimes offer, a place of beautiful forgetting alongside many more of wilful neglect and destruction (OS Landranger Map No.149: SO 524 460)